# Retro Barbecue

Linda Everett

# Retro

# Barbecue

*Tasty Recipes for the Grillin' Guy*

COLLECTORS PRESS

PORTLAND, OREGON

Copyright © 2002 Collectors Press, Inc.

Library of Congress Cataloging-in-Publication Data

Everett, Linda, 1946-
    The retro barbecue : tasty recipes for the grillin' guy /
by Linda Everett.— 1st American ed.
        p. cm.
    ISBN 1-888054-63-8 (hardcover)
    1. Barbecue cookery.    I. Title.
TX840.B3 E9424 2002
641.7'6–dc21

2001005390

Design: Trina Stahl
Editor: Brenda Koplin

Printed in Singapore.
First American edition
9 8 7 6 5 4 3 2 1

Collectors Press books are available at special discounts
for bulk purchases, premiums, and promotions. Special
editions, including personalized inserts or covers, and
corporate logos, can be printed in quantity for special
purposes. For further information contact: Special Sales,
Collectors Press, Inc., P.O. Box 230986, Portland, OR
97281. Toll-free: 1-800-423-1848

For a free catalog write: Collectors Press, Inc., P.O. Box
230986, Portland, OR 97281. Toll-free: 1-800-423-1848 or
visit our website at: www.collectorspress.com

# Contents

# Introduction

The 1950s saw an age of casserole cooking, molded salads at every potluck and the comfort food we Americans love. Eisenhower had won double-u double-u two in the 1940s and while he was president in the 1950s we felt safe and successful. America was in boomtown time and those ex-frontline GIs wanted the picket-fenced house, a car in the garage, and a patio with a barbecue. Never mind a few troublemakers like that Elvis kid, the 1950s was June Cleaver in her pearls passing the 'burgers to Dad at the grill.

Yes, Dad was the master of the flame, singeing his eyebrows while smoking out the neighbors. *Ozzie and Harriet*, the Beaver, *Life with Father* and Lucy all knew who could handle the manly skills of throwing real food on the grill and doin' it right.

Although we no longer feel that barbecuing is a totally male-oriented expertise, it's still pretty much their territory. I have many

mental pictures of the men in my family flippin' those burgers, slopping on aromatic sauce and bravely standing in the drifting smoke. My brother Ron is a true grill master, tested by flare-ups, branded by embers, tried by and thousands of plebian 'burgers masterfully cooked on his huge barrel grill.

The equipment today ranges from the old Weber kettle to picnic hibachis to gigantic affairs that look like a space shuttle in cast iron and chrome. Still, there's an art to getting the coals just right, in how many chips of mesquite to sprinkle on the flame. It takes an eye, a feel, for the right amount of time before turning that juicy burger and just how much of your favorite homemade sauce to brush on and when. Whether you grill on your tiny apartment porches, on the beach among sand dunes and fireworks, or on your own deck by the pool, there's plainly nothing like the taste and the 1950s homeyness of a barbecue meal with family and friends.

So, jump in here barbecuer whether you've seared and grilled half a steer over a pickup load of charcoal over the years, or your experience is limited to a few 'dogs on the picnic hibachi. The following pages cover the basics for the novice as well as more than a few new, yet not bizarre,

The average American could build their own Cape Cod cottage for $3,500 by using a do-it-yourself guide by Hubbard Cobb published in 1951.

recipes and ideas to interest the skilled craftsman. Take the challenge, tie on that apron declaring you "King of the Grill" and dive into the savory smoke from your favorite barbecue grill.

# Fire 'N' Fuel

To add that certain unmistakable woodsy campfire flavor, use dampened chips from any of a number of sweet and nonresinous woods. Choose your favorite hardwood such as hickory, oak, maple, or alder. Fruit or nut trees, especially apple, also provide sweetness. Avoid any fir or pine chips as the sap is bitter. For a different and delectable taste try tossing a few cloves of garlic into the fire.

Of course your main fire will be of charcoal, briquettes and/or gas-fired. Wood is wonderful but it takes forever to burn down to the desired hot coals. Briquettes are often made from fruit pits or hardwoods, which is a great start for flavor. For a small portable hibachi or picnic grill 12 to 24 briquettes are all that's needed. For a larger home grill or large patio barbecue expect to use 30 to 40. If you plan to cook a large roast or a whole turkey, add more fuel as the coals burn down. Do this by lining the new briquettes along the outer edge of the burning ones and use a poker to push them into the hot coals as needed.

## Lightin' the Fire

Do this 30 minutes before you want to grill your main course. If using charcoal or briquettes, stack them in a pyramid, pour just enough odorless fluid over to dampen the briquettes or charcoal. This is about ½ cup fluid for 30 to 40 briquettes. Let stand for 2 or 3 minutes, then light. When the briquettes have white ash forming, spread them out and adjust the grill.

Judging the temperature of your charcoal blaze is a combination of experience and some well used rules of thumb. A low fire (approximately 275°) is when you can hold your hand at grill level for 4 seconds, a medium blaze (approximately 300°) for 3 seconds, and a 2-second test is a fast fire at about 325° to 350°.

Unless you want charring from flare-ups (due to fat dripping into the fire or from oils in your sauce), keep a spray bottle filled with water on hand. Lightly spritz those high flyin' flames so they don't make your main course look and taste like charred cow pies.

## Grill Time

**Beef steaks** (1 inch thick)
rare–8 to 12 minutes
medium–12 to 15 minutes
well done–15 to 20 minutes

**Beef steaks** (1½ inches thick)
rare–10 to 15 minutes
medium–14 to 18 minutes
well done–18 to 25 minutes

**Lamb chops and steaks** (1 inch thick)
medium rare–6 to 14 minutes
well done–18 to 25 minutes

**Lamb chops and steaks** (1½ inches thick)
medium rare–8 to 16 minutes
well done–20 to 30 minutes

**Chicken**
split halves–25 to 45 minutes
pieces–5 to 8 minutes per side

**Hamburgers**
rare–10 to 12 minutes (not recommended due to danger of E-Coli)
medium–14 to 15 minutes (still not safe)
well done–18 to 20 minutes (juices run clear; about 160°)

**Ham steaks**
1 inch thick–30 to 35 minutes
1½ inches thick–35 to 45 minutes

**Fish steaks**
1 inch thick–6 to 9 minutes
1½ inches thick–8 to 12 minutes

# Tools 'N' Stuff You'll Need

**1.** A meat thermometer is a good investment for both your kitchen and your grill feast. Most meats should read at least 160° to be safe.

**2.** Gloves are sure handy, especially the thick fire-resistant kind.

**3.** Long-handled basting brush, mop or even a small paint brush for sloshing on that luscious delectable sauce.

**4.** Tongs work much better than a fork on chicken, hot dogs, veggies, and more. Stabbing steaks or roasts with a big fork means releasing the nice juices you definitely want to keep in. Don't go cheap. A good quality stainless steel long-handled set of tongs will last through years of turnings.

**5.** To keep your grill clean and to scrape off those bits of unknown charred gunk, get a wire brush. The best ones have sturdy brass bristles.

**6.** For shish kabobs, keep on hand bamboo or stainless skewers. Soak the bamboo ones in water overnight before using.

**7.** If you want to grill fish, such as trout or other goodies that would fall to pieces if turned with a spatula, get yourself a wire-hinged basket made just for this purpose.

**8.** A long-handled spatula for flipping those burgers and other delights. As with the barbecuing tongs, go for a good stainless steel one.

# The Marinades

A good marinade can make that bargain cut of beef chuck or shoulder steak into a tender, memorable meal. This is especially handy when you're trying to feed a crowd without going bankrupt. Try out these marinade recipes then get creative and experiment with your own favorite ingredients. Remember, the acid of wine, vinegar or lemon juice helps to break down the fibers of the cut and works as a tenderizer. If you buy a commercial tenderizer in powdered form, get one without salt as an ingredient. If you do use a tenderizer with salt it will draw out the juices in the meat and ruin the balance of the barbecue sauce spices.

Mix ingredients together in a glass or other container that won't be affected by the acids. It should be slightly larger than the cut of meat. Always discard the marinade after use and move on to your sauce to baste the centerpiece of your barbecue feast.

# Pistol Pete's Marinade

½ cup oil (olive is best, vegetable is okay—
    same in all recipes)

3 tblsps lemon juice (use the real thing—same
    in all recipes)

½ cup white wine

½ tsp salt (or to taste)

½ tsp coarse ground pepper (fresh ground is
    best—same in all recipes)

1 large sweet onion, finely chopped

"Betty Crocker"
was actually
forty-eight women
who made up the
General Mills
Home Service
Department.

# Monterey Bay Marinade

½ cup oil

1 tblsp vinegar

½ cup dry red wine (or try Burgundy)

1 small onion, minced

1 tblsp chopped parsley (fresh if possible—same
    in all recipes)

1 carrot, minced

1 bay leaf

½ tsp salt

½ tsp coarsely ground pepper

# Kettle Falls Marinade

½ cup oil

1½ cups water

1 5-oz bottle soy sauce (low salt is okay)

¼ cup brown sugar, packed

2 tsps Worcestershire sauce

1 tblsp lemon juice

¼ cup bourbon or brandy (optional)

# Sunsetview Marinade

½ cup oil

½ cup red wine

3 tblsps tarragon vinegar

2 cloves garlic, crushed (smash flat with
a knife)

1 bay leaf

1 small onion, sliced thinly

1 tblsp minced parsley

15–20 whole peppercorns, crushed

# Honolulu Lulu's Marinade

2 tsps honey
1 tsp powdered ginger
½ cup sherry
½ tsp salt
2–3 cloves garlic, minced (to your taste)
1 medium onion, finely chopped
1 cup soy sauce

· S.O.S cleans blackened pots

# Canadian Rockies Moose Marinade

3 medium onions, finely chopped
   (any good old yellow onions will do)
1 cup green onions, finely chopped
   (green part and all)
1½ carrots, scraped and finely chopped
⅔ cup celery, finely chopped
5 cups dry white wine
¾ cup tarragon vinegar
2 cloves garlic, crushed
2 bay leaves
2 tsps salt
1 tsp coarsely ground black pepper

Okay, so this sounds exotic, but you hunters out there will love this for your venison, moose, elk or bear. It has enough tasty ingredients to cut back on that gamey flavor, while the vinegar and wine tenderize that 8-point grandpappy buck. If you're going to cook a bear roast be sure you remove absolutely all fat to avoid the rank flavor it contains.

**1.** In a large saucepan combine the onions, carrots, celery, wine, vinegar, garlic, bay, salt, and pepper. Simmer for 5 minutes. Cool.

**2.** In a glass or stainless pan place the steaks or whatever and pour over the marinade. The meat should be completely covered.

Refrigerate for 2 or 3 days. Discard marinade and grill the meat according to directions. Remember, wild game usually has very little fat, so don't kill it on the grill. You might want to consider basting with one of the flavored butters.

# The Sauce!

From the cowboy barbecue of Texas to the year-round grillin' of California, the sauce is the secret. There's as much argument, probably more, over the right barbecue sauce as there is the perfect fire. Try these variations, then get brave and experiment with your own special combination.

# Rodeo Cowboy Sauce

**T**his sauce looks complicated and time consuming; okay, so it is. It's worth it.

**4 cups rich beef broth (homemade is best, if possible)**
**1 bay leaf**
**1 tsp dried oregano**

In a large kettle bring the beef broth, bay leaf, and oregano to a boil, then reduce to a simmer.

While broth mixture is simmering, melt 3 tblsps butter (unsalted) in a heavy skillet. Add in:

**½ cup chopped onions**
**¼ cup chopped celery**
**¼ cup chopped green pepper**
**¼ cup minced garlic**
**2 tblsps Tejas BBQ Rub, (recipe to follow)**
**½ tsp salt**
**½ tsp coarse ground pepper**
**¼–½ tsp cayenne (according to how hot you like your sauce)**

Stir this mixture over medium-high heat until lightly browned, about 5 minutes.

Stir the following into the kettle of broth mixture:

**3 tblsps soy sauce**
**2 tblsps lemon juice**
**3 tblsps apple cider vinegar**

Back in that skillet, brown 1 pound lean hickory-smoked bacon and cut it up into small pieces, drain, and add to the pot of simmering broth.

Continue simmering, stirring occasionally, until the sauce is thick; about an hour.

# Semi-Cheatin' Sauce

¼ cup catsup

¼ cup dark molasses

1 cup smoke-flavored barbecue sauce

2 tblsps apple cider vinegar

2 tsps Worcestershire sauce

½ tsp Tabasco sauce (or similar hot sauce)

1 tsp dry mustard

2 tblsps lemon juice

4 tblsps oil

Combine all ingredients in a medium saucepan and bring to a simmer. Continue cooking over low heat for 10 minutes.

**Walt Disney's *Davy Crockett* TV series brought on an enthusiasm for Early American decor in every suburban home.**

# Deeper South Sauce

2 cups tomato sauce

3 tblsps tomato paste

4 tblsps dark molasses

½ cup apple cider vinegar

¼ cup dark brown sugar, firmly packed

2–4 drops Tabasco sauce (to taste)

1 tblsp dry mustard

¼ cup Worcestershire sauce

1 jalapeño pepper, minced (or equal amount from canned)

½ cup crushed pineapple or equal amount apricot preserves

Combine all ingredients together thoroughly except the fruit. Stir in the fruit and taste. Add more of the hot sauce if desired.

# Independence Day Firecracker Sauce

**3 tblsps vegetable oil**
**1 medium onion, thinly sliced**
**4 cloves garlic, chopped**

In a medium-sized heavy saucepan, heat the oil and cook the onion until clear, but not brown. Add in the garlic and cook for one minute longer. Stir often.

To the above add the following:

**1 cup orange juice**
**¼ cup lemon juice**
**6 tblsps red wine vinegar**
**½ cup water**
**¼ cup honey**
**¼ cup dark brown sugar**
**(firmly packed)**
**2 tblsps liquid smoke flavoring**
**3 tblsps finely chopped ginger**
**2–4 drops Tabasco sauce**
**(to your taste)**
**2 tblsps chili powder**
**½ tsp salt**
**1 tblsp dry mustard**

Bring to a gentle boil, then reduce to low and cook for approximately an hour. Stir often. Sauce should be thick and smooth. If you want a smoother sauce, remove and discard the onion and garlic with a slotted spoon. Cool and refrigerate. Makes about 5 cups that will keep for two weeks.

# High Ponderosa Sauce

**8 cups barbecue sauce (store-bought bottled**
**is okay, but homemade is better)**
**1 bottle (12 ounces) beer**
**1 bottle (about 14 ounces) catsup**
**1 medium onion, finely chopped**
**1 clove garlic, thinly sliced**
**1 tsp dried hot red peppers**
**1½ tblsps brown sugar**
**1 tsp salt**

# Tejas ("Te-haas") BBQ Rub

**2 tsps garlic powder**

**1 tsp crumbled bay leaf (about one leaf)**

**¾ tsp salt (adjust this to your own taste)**

**¾ tsp coarse ground black pepper**

**2½ tblsps brown sugar (dark)**

**2 tblsps paprika**

**2 tsps onion powder**

**1½ tsps dried sweet basil**

**⅛ tsp ground cumin**

**2 tsps dry mustard**

**¾ tsp ground coriander**

**¾ tsp dried thyme**

In some parts of the country, mainly Texas and the south, the meat is rubbed down with this mix of spices before throwing it on the grill. It also works well as an ingredient in barbecue sauce (see above). The rub will keep for up to four months in a sealed container without refrigeration.

Using this spicy mixture is easy. Simply rub it into the meat the night before (I recommend using disposable kitchen gloves), then cover the ribs or steak or whatever in plastic wrap and leave in the refrigerator until you're ready to fling it on that perfect grillin' fire.

# The Rest of the Meal

That great piece of barbecued beef, chicken, pork, or fish needs something equally delicious to fill up the rest of the plate. These traditional side dishes bring the crowd to the table for seconds and maybe even thirds.

After signing a recording contract with RCA, Elvis took his bonus and bought his non-driving mother a candy pink Fleetwood sedan Caddy.

# Chilis

Americans love their chili and there are thousands of chili cookoffs around these great states. Because of the obvious influence from our neighbors in Mexico we must give them some credit for the spicy mix. However, the U.S. Southwest has certainly taken it to a higher level using imagination and a Don Quixote quest for the perfect recipe. Some chili aficionados say it's a travesty to add beans to the pot. Others swear that tomatoes in any form are a big no-no. The meat can range from beef chuck to loin of venison; even raccoon, possum, armadillo, emu, or other exotic creatures have shown up in the savory concoction. Have fun with your chili and continue to fine-tune it for your family's tastes.

For any recipe calling for fresh or dried chili peppers (not the powder) wear kitchen or disposable gloves. The oils will burn your hands. And for Pete's sake never touch your face or eyes when handling these delicious, but demonic, little gems.

# Hot Shot Chili

¼ up old-fashioned beef lard (yes, it's sinful, but there's nothing like the flavor)

3 large sweet onions, chopped

3 medium green peppers, chopped

4 cups cooked pinto beans (Okay, if you want to make the real thing you are not allowed to use canned. But if time is short, I give you clandestine permission.) See recipe for beans below if you want to be a genuine chilimaster.

1 cup finely chopped hot peppers (How hot? Jalapeños if you want to be cautious; Habañeros if you want to risk your life! All sorts in between.)

1 quart tomato juice (48-ounce can)

2 pounds lean ground beef, browned and drained of fat

2 tsps cumin seeds

1½ tsps salt

½ tsp coarsely ground pepper

2 tsps chili powder

3 large cloves of garlic, minced

1 can (16 ounces) whole tomatoes or chunk style

**1.** In a skillet melt the beef lard and gently cook the onions and green peppers. Do not brown. Drain on paper towels. Add in beans.

**2.** Stir in the hot peppers, tomato juice, cooked ground beef, cumin, salt, ground pepper, chili powder, garlic and whole tomatoes.

**3.** Simmer, uncovered, for 3 hours. Stir occasionally.

**4.** Serve with big chunks of sourdough bread and a green salad.

In the '50s, TV variety show host, Ed Sullivan, defined American culture. It ranged from opera to Elvis.

22

# Yee-hah! Lasso Them Doggies!

3½ cups boiling water

8 dried hot red chilies

½ pound beef suet

3 pounds lean beef chuck, cut into
    ½-inch cubes

3 medium-sized bay leaves

1 tblsp ground cumin

6 cloves garlic, chopped

3 tsps dried oregano

3 tblsps paprika

1 tblsp sugar

1 tblsp salt

3 tblsps cornmeal

1 tsp cayenne (optional)

cooked pinto beans (see recipe below)

**1.** Pour hot water over the chilies in a medium bowl. Let soak for 30 to 45 minutes. Strain the liquid through a sieve and save. Set the chilies aside.

**2.** In a heavy 5- to 6-quart pot cook the suet over medium heat, stirring often. Remove the suet bits and save ¼ cup of the rendered fat.

**3.** Add the beef to the pot and cook until the meat is lightly browned.

**4.** Add 2½ cups of the chili liquid and bring it to a boil. Add in the bay leaves and reduce to low.

**5.** Simmer for 1 hour.

**6.** Add in the cumin, the red chilies, the remaining chili water, garlic, oregano, paprika, sugar and salt.

**7.** Simmer for 30 minutes. Slowly stir in the cornmeal to thicken.

**8.** Taste the chili and add cayenne to taste if needed.

**9.** Serve with the chili beans in a separate bowl. Cooked long-grain rice is also nice to spoon this over.

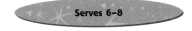

Serves 6–8

# Traditional Pinto Beans

1 pound dried pinto beans (2 cups)
6 cups water
1 medium bay leaf
1 medium onion, peeled but not cut
1 tsp salt

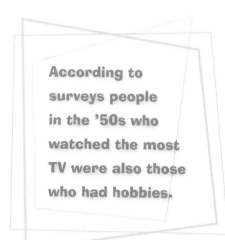

According to surveys people in the '50s who watched the most TV were also those who had hobbies.

**1.** Wash the pinto beans and pick out any blemished ones or debris.

**2.** Pour the beans into a heavy 3- or 4-quart saucepan.

**3.** Add the water, bay leaf and onion. Bring to a boil over high heat.

**4.** Reduce to a simmer and cook for 4 hours. Stir occasionally. If you need to add more liquid be sure it's hot or it'll toughen up the beans.

**5.** Add the salt and continue cooking for another 30 minutes.

**6.** Using a slotted spoon, pick out the bay leaf. Drain the beans and serve.

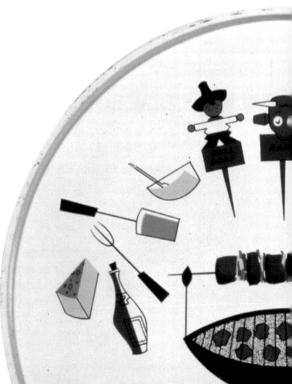

# Pedernales River Ranch Chili

3 tblsps vegetable oil

3½ to 4 pounds lean ground beef chuck
    or venison

2 medium or 1 large onion, coarsely
    chopped

2 cloves garlic, finely chopped

1 tsp dried oregano (not ground)

1 tsp ground cumin

2 tblsps chili powder (or to your taste)

1 tsp salt

3 to 6 drops Tabasco sauce (to your taste)
    or your favorite hot sauce

2½ cups water

1½ cups canned crushed tomatoes

**1.** Over medium heat, in a heavy kettle or Dutch oven, add oil and brown the meat with the onion and garlic.

**2.** Add in oregano, cumin, chili powder, salt, hot sauce, water and tomatoes. Bring to a boil, then turn down to a gentle simmer.

**3.** Simmer uncovered, stirring occasionally, for about 30 minutes more.

**4.** Skim off any excess fat and check if you need to add more hot sauce or chili powder.

**5.** Ladle into bowls and serve with crusty bread or soda crackers.

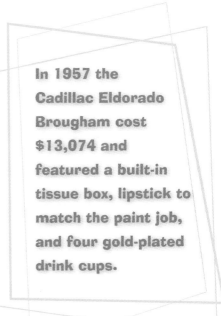

In 1957 the Cadillac Eldorado Brougham cost $13,074 and featured a built-in tissue box, lipstick to match the paint job, and four gold-plated drink cups.

# Sunset Boulevard Bowl-of-Red

½ pound dried pinto beans (cook as directed)

3 tblsps vegetable oil

3 medium green bell peppers, cored, seeded and coarsely chopped

5 cups crushed tomatoes, canned is okay

3 large onions, coarsely chopped

3 cloves garlic, finely chopped

½ cup parsley, fresh, finely chopped

1 stick butter (½ cup)

2½ pounds lean ground beef

1 pound lean ground pork (not sausage)

3 to 5 tblsps chili powder (according to taste)

1½ tsps ground cumin

1½ tsps black pepper

2 tblsps salt

**1.** In a large heavy skillet heat the vegetable oil and cook the green peppers for about 5 minutes. Add in the onions and cook until clear, about another 5 to 8 minutes. Stir in garlic and parsley and set aside.

**2.** In a separate skillet melt butter over medium heat and add in the beef and pork. Cook, stirring often, until the meat is browned. Add in the onion mixture and stir in the chili powder. Cook another 10 minutes, stirring occasionally.

**3.** Add meat mixture to the beans and stir in the cumin, black pepper and salt. Bring to a boil, then reduce to a simmer and cover. Stir occasionally. Simmer for 1 hour.

**4.** Remove cover and continue simmering for another 30 minutes.

**5.** Skim fat from chili and ladle into bowls.

Serves 6 to 8

## BEST FOODS . . .

In 1953 *Esquire* magazine published a gentlemen's guide to outdoor hospitality, or barbecue etiquette.

# Boston Harbor Baked Beans

4 cups navy or pea beans

1½ tsps salt

3 tblsps brown sugar

½ cup molasses

½ pound salt pork (as lean as you
  can find)

I don't know about you, but a barbecue isn't a barbecue without real home-made baked beans. Whenever we have a family get-together at my brother's beach cabin I bring this traditional dish. It goes well with just about anything you slap on the grill; from hot dogs to 'burgers to T-bones to ribs. The sweet rich flavor of the oven-baked beans truly sets off the smoky tang of barbecued meats.

**Our family loves this with Classic Beantown Brown Bread (recipe follows), but grilled sourdough or any other crusty bread is great for soaking up the delectable "sop" from these beans.**

**1.** Follow directions for cleaning beans. Cover with cool water and soak overnight.

**2.** The next day drain the beans, add fresh water to cover and bring to a boil over high heat. Then lower the heat and simmer gently until the skins start to flake off.

**3.** Remove from the heat and drain. Save the liquid.

**4.** Stir the salt, sugar, and molasses into 1 cup of the reserved bean liquid. Stir until the sugar dissolves.

**5.** Cut the salt pork into 1-inch cubes and place half in the bottom of a bean pot. (You need a real bean pot to make this right, but I suppose a heavy ceramic oven-safe dish with a lid will do. Another great alternative is a well-seasoned Dutch oven.) Pour beans over the pork, add the salt and sugar mixture, then poke the remaining salt pork into the top layer. If your salt pork is especially fatty you can render out some of the lard by cooking the cubes over medium heat for a few minutes. Don't overcook or you'll lose

that special taste the salt pork gives the beans.

**6.** If needed, add more of the bean liquid to cover. Place lid on bean pot and bake at 275° for 8 hours or longer. (Do not discard bean liquid.) I like to cook mine all night.

**7.** Check beans from time to time (yes, I drag myself out to the kitchen at about 3:00 A.M.) and add more of the reserved liquid if needed to keep the beans moist. During the last hour or so of baking remove the lid and allow the beans to brown a little.

Serves 6 to 8

## Vermonters Version

**Leave out the brown sugar and molasses. Instead, add in ½ cup real maple syrup. Put a medium peeled whole sweet onion in the bottom of the bean pot before filling it with beans.**

# Classic Beantown Brown Bread

1 cup rye flour
1 cup yellow cornmeal
1 cup white flour
2 tsps baking soda
1 tsp salt
¾ cup dark molasses
2 cups buttermilk
1 cup raisins (optional)

**1.** In a large bowl mix together the rye flour, cornmeal, and white flour.

**2.** Blend in baking soda and salt.

**3.** Stir molasses and buttermilk into dry ingredients. Add in raisins if you like them (I do). Do not beat.

**4.** Pour batter into ⅔ of a clean greased and floured one-pound coffee can or use a mold.

**5.** Cover can tightly with aluminum foil.

**6.** Steam 3 to 3½ hours on a rack in a kettle with a tight-fitting lid. Use only 3 or 4 inches of water. I like to use a canning pressure cooker without the little cap that holds in the steam. This way I can cook several at one time. This bread freezes well.

Spread generously with good butter or honey butter.

**Makes 8 to 10 servings**

# Yuppie Cheater Beans

**4 cans (28 ounces) good quality pork and beans**
**12 slices lean thick-sliced bacon, cooked crisp and cut into ¼-inch pieces**
**¾ cup firmly packed brown sugar**
**1⅓ cups catsup**
**2 tsps dry mustard**
**2 medium onions, finely chopped**

Here's a little quicker and easier way to yummy baked beans. You'll still get the compliments and it won't take all day (or night).

**1.** In a large bowl mix together the beans, bacon, sugar, catsup, mustard, and chopped onions.

**2.** Spoon into a 3- to 4-quart oiled baking dish. Bake at 350°, uncovered, for about 1½ to 2 hours or until beans are bubbly. Stir occasionally.

Serves 10 to 12

# Dottie's "Deetroit" Beans

**1 pound dried Great Northern beans**
**6 cups water**
**2 tsps salt**
**1 tsp dry mustard**
**1 large onion, finely chopped**
**⅓ cup dark molasses**
**½ cup firmly packed dark brown sugar**
**½ cup bottled chili sauce**
**2⅓ cups tomatoes (1 pound 3-ounce size can), chunk style**
**½ pound thick-sliced lean smoky bacon; try the maple flavored for a change**

**1.** In a large pot cover the beans with water and bring to a boil; boil for 3 minutes. Cover pot and let stand for an hour.

**2.** Put beans back on low heat and let simmer until tender, about 1½ hours.

**3.** Drain and reserve liquid from beans.

**4.** Mix in salt, mustard, onion, molasses, brown sugar, chili sauce, and tomatoes. Pour into a shallow oiled baking pan.

**5.** Cut bacon strips into quarters and arrange atop the beans.

**6.** Bake in oven at 300° for 2 hours. Add more of the reserved bean liquid as needed to keep them from drying out.

Serves 6

# Eat Your Veggies!

Vegetables usually get the blech! comment, especially from the kids. That's because they seem to fall at the bottom of the list on taste and creativity. These recipes have nothing strange that will make your family or guests raise their eyebrows in suspicion. Nothing here but yum!

# Sauvie ("saw-vee") Island Summertime Corn

**1 fat ear or 2 small ears of corn per person**
**½ cup butter, olive oil or vegetable oil. Try flavored oils for a variation, even the flavored sprays.**

Sauvie Island is a real place. A large island in the Columbia River close to Portland, Oregon, it has the charm of pioneer history, with bountiful soil from the flooding river. Sauvie is mostly small truck farms where luscious summer veggies can be bought, or if you're energetic you can go for the "U-Pick." The corn is sweet and the scenery is sublime.

**1.** Pull off the dry outer husks until you get to the tender light green inner ones; leave these on. Save a few husks and tear into ¼" strips and set aside.

**2.** Pull the inner husks back gently and remove the silk.

**3.** Baste the ears with butter or oil, then close and tie with the reserved strips.

**4.** Cool by immersing in cold water for 15 to 30 minutes.

**5.** Drain well.

**6.** Place on a lightly greased grill about 4 to 6 inches above the coals.

**7.** Cook, turning often, for 15 to 20 minutes. Corn husks should be streaked with brown.

# Onions You Will Cry For!

heavy-duty foil
1 Walla Walla Sweet, Vidalia, Maui
    Sweet or other mild-flavored onion
    per person
melted butter
thyme, oregano, rosemary, or tarragon
    (optional)

**1.** Tear off a sheet of foil big enough to wrap the entire onion.

**2.** Place onion in center of foil and baste generously with butter.

**3.** Sprinkle with spices of your choice.

**4.** Pull foil up around the onion and place about 4 to 6 inches over the coals.

**5.** Grill for about 15 to 20 minutes. Test for tenderness by opening the foil and poking the onion with a skewer or knife.

The '50s queen of tv housewife commercials was Betty Furness. In her classic black dress and pearls she demonstrated Westinghouse vacuum cleaners to admiring fans.

# King O' the Forest Mushrooms

2 to 3 large (2½ to 3 inch diameter)
    mushrooms per person; white, brown,
    or your own personal favorite
½ cup melted butter, olive oil, or
    flavored oil
thyme, oregano, rosemary or tarragon

**1.** Cut off the stem of the mushrooms.

**2.** Baste with butter (or oil) and sprinkle with your choice of spices (optional)

**3.** Grill about 4 or 6 inches from the coals. Turn often. Cooking time is about 10 minutes.

# Veggies-on-a-Stick

10 small boiling onions
5 small pattypan summer squash or 5
     1½-inch chunks of zucchini
2 large sweet red peppers
½ tsp salt
¼ tsp coarsely ground pepper
¼ tsp garlic powder
¼ cup melted butter

**1.** Boil onions in a small amount of water for about 25 minutes, or until nearly tender.

**2.** If you use pattypan squash cut it into quarters. Cut the peppers into large squares.

**3.** Mix together the salt, pepper, and garlic powder. Roll the vegetables in the spice mixture.

**4.** On skewers alternate squash, onion, then peppers.

**5.** Grill vegetables over medium heat for 20 to 25 minutes or until tender. Turn often and baste with the melted butter.

# Redhouse on the River's Potatoes

1 pound new red or white potatoes
3 tsps olive oil (or other mild-flavored oil)
1 tsp dried rosemary
½ tsp salt
¼ tsp coarsely ground black pepper
dash of cayenne pepper
½ tsp garlic powder

**1.** Slice potatoes into wedges.

**2.** In a medium bowl combine the oil, rosemary, salt, peppers, and garlic. Mix together well.

**3.** Add potatoes to the oil mixture and toss to coat.

**4.** Place potatoes in a wire basket, heavy foil, or on a grill rack

**5.** Grill about 4 inches from a medium fire for about 25 minutes or until golden brown.

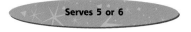

Serves 5 or 6

Eat Your

# Dressed-Up Fries in a Pouch

**Heavy-duty aluminum foil**
**Packaged french fries, partially thawed;**
    **one fat handful per person**
**oil or vegetable spray (try one of the**
    **flavored variety)**
**garlic powder**
**parsley**
**cayenne pepper (optional)**
**salt**
**coarsely ground black pepper**

**1.** Tear off a square of foil. Place handful of fries in center.

**2.** Sprinkle fries with oil, garlic, parsley, a dash of cayenne, salt and black pepper.

**3.** Gather up the foil into a pouch but leave a gap at the top for steam to escape.

**4.** Place on the barbecue grate, shaking the pouch occasionally, and cook for about 15 minutes. Should be done when package is hot to the touch.

**5.** Serve with your best 'burgers and the following sauce.

**The 1954 Secretary of Health, Education, and Welfare advised the American public that hobbies were essential to national happiness.**

# Fry Sauce

**1 part mayonnaise (the good stuff)**
**1 part catsup**
**¼ tsp garlic powder**
**½ tsp parsley**

**1.** In a small bowl combine the mayonnaise, catsup, garlic and parsley.

**2.** Serve with the grilled fries above.

# South Hills Potato and Onion Bake

**Heavy-duty foil**
**3 large Russet potatoes**
**2 large sweet onions (try to get Walla Wallas, Visalia, or Maui Sweets, if you can)**
**1 tsp salt**
**½ tsp paprika**
**½ tsp coarsely ground pepper**
**¼ cup butter, melted**

**1.** Tear off 6 18-inch squares of heavy-duty foil

**2.** Cut the potatoes and onions into thick slices. Divide equally into the 6 foil squares.

**3.** Sprinkle each helping of potatoes with the salt, paprika, pepper, and butter.

**4.** Seal up the squares leaving a small opening for steam.

**5.** Grill over coals for about 1 hour, turning the packets several times.

Try adding in other veggies like carrots, mushrooms, squash, etc.

The first handheld-size transistor radios made their impact on the market in 1959.

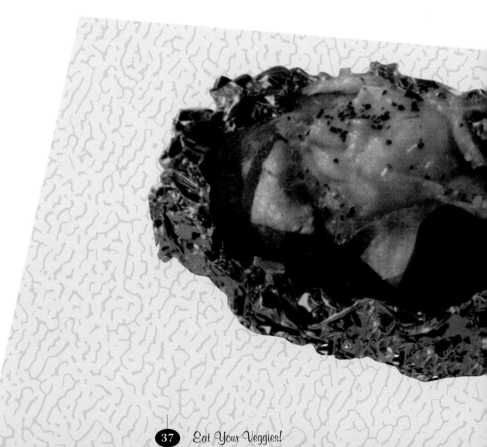

# Tasty Ribs

From the smoky brick pits of the south to the big portable grills on a city corner, to the backyard set-ups, ribs are the ultimate test. Chefs pass their rub and sauce secrets on to the next generation. While standing in the rich, savory smoke, long-handled tongs in one hand, basting mop in the other, the dilemmas of life are mulled over, cussed, and discussed. Ah, an American classic!

## Basic cookin'

Start your spareribs bone-side down. Toss a few dampened chips on the coals and if you have a hood on your barbecue, close it. Turn ribs occasionally and start basting both sides of the ribs the last 30 minutes. Time depends on how hot your fire is, but you can expect 2 to 2½ hours. Resist the temptation to use the marinade the meat has been relaxing in. It isn't safe.

# Put-on-Your-Bib Ribs

10 pounds pork ribs (the small end)
2 quarts water
1 large onion, chopped
2 cloves garlic, thinly chopped
¼ cup liquid hickory smoke
1½ tblsps salt
1 tblsp coarsely ground pepper
1 tsp onion salt
½ tsp paprika

**1.** Remove any excess fat or tissue from the ribs.

**2.** In a stockpot combine the water, onion, garlic, liquid smoke, salt, pepper, onion salt, and paprika.

**3.** Add ribs and marinate overnight in refrigerator. Discard marinade.

**4.** Grill as described above using your favorite sauce.

# Bad Billy's Best Ribs

10 pounds beef or pork spareribs
1 cup apple cider vinegar
2 tblsps cayenne pepper
5 tblsps celery salt
½ cup salt
2 tsps ground cumin
¼ cup coarse ground black pepper

**1.** Rub the meat thoroughly with vinegar until it is moistened.

**2.** Rub the spice mixture into the meat, getting every surface covered well.

**3.** Cook as described above.

# Maui Wowee Luau Ribs

1 tblsp ginger root (about a 1-inch piece),
    crushed with a knife

1 large clove garlic, crushed with a knife

½ cup soy sauce

½ cup white sugar

½ cup brown sugar

½ cup catsup

2 tblsps sherry

1 tsp salt

8 pounds pork back ribs

**1.** In a bowl mix together the crushed ginger, garlic, soy sauce, sugars, catsup, sherry, and salt.

**2.** Rub mixture into the meat. Pour a little over the top and discard. Place meat in a glass or stainless pan and cover. Refrigerate for at least 3 hours.

**3.** Cook as described above.

In the early '50s artist Jackson Pollock shocked art critics with his drip and dribble style of painting.

# Bart's Backyard Ribs

1 cup smoke-flavored bottled barbecue
    sauce (okay, so it's cheatin')

¼ cup dark molasses

4 tblsps butter

2 tblsps lemon juice

2 tblsps apple cider vinegar

1 tsp dry mustard

3 tsps Worcestershire sauce

½ to 1 tsp Tabasco sauce (according to
    your taste)

4 to 5 pounds pork loin back ribs

**1.** In a saucepan combine barbecue sauce, molasses, butter, lemon juice, vinegar, mustard, Worcestershire sauce, and Tabasco. Simmer 10 minutes.

**2.** Cook ribs as described above.

# Boathouse Ribs

5 pounds pork spareribs, cut into
    4-inch pieces
1 quart apple cider vinegar
1 cup firmly packed brown sugar
1 tsp salt
1 tsp coarsely ground black pepper
¼ tsp paprika
¼ tsp cayenne pepper
2 to 3 large cloves garlic, crushed with
    a knife

**1.** Rinse the rib sections in cold water and drain well.

**2.** In a large glass or enameled pan pour the vinegar and gently stir in the brown sugar, salt, black pepper, paprika, cayenne, and garlic.

**3.** Add in ribs, turning to cover well with the mixture and marinade overnight in the refrigerator.

**4.** Before grilling the next day, baste again well with the marinade and cook as described above.

# One Last Rib Recipe

3 pounds beef back ribs (as meaty as
   you can find)

water

2 tsps oil

½ cup chopped green onions

5 cloves garlic, finely chopped

½ cup apple cider vinegar

¼ cup creamy-style peanut butter (try
   chunky too)

⅓ cup dark molasses

3 tblsps Worcestershire sauce

¼ cup soy sauce (low sodium is okay)

dash of cayenne pepper

In 1950 only 21
percent of the
American public
owned a television
set. By 1955
that number had
jumped to 66
percent.

There are so many wonderful and taste-satisfying rib recipes. I added in this one because it has a different, sort of Thai flavor. Don't be scared off by the untraditional peanut butter.

**1.** Rinse and dry ribs.

**2.** Place ribs in a Dutch oven (or similar deep heavy pot) and cover with the water. Bring to a boil over medium heat. Cover, remove from heat and let stand for about 30 minutes.

**3.** While meat is cooking, heat the oil in a skillet and add in the onions. Cook, stirring often, for about 3 minutes.

**4.** Add in the garlic and continue to cook for 1 minute longer.

**5.** Stir in the vinegar, peanut butter, molasses, Worcestershire, soy sauce, and cayenne. Cook this mixture until it starts to thicken, about 10 minutes. Remove from the heat.

**6.** Place ribs over medium fire and grill according to above general directions. Baste generously with the sauce the last 20 minutes.

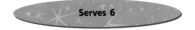

Serves 6

# Superb Sizzlin' Steaks

The key with steak is not to overcook it so it becomes a tough, dry, tasteless slab of boot sole. Piercing it often with your long-handled turning fork will allow those tasty juices to disappear into the fire and ruin your barbecue masterpiece.

The best cuts for grilling are rib, T-bone, sirloin, club, or porterhouse cut 1 to 2 inches thick. These can be soaked in a marinade if you want a particular flavor, but it isn't necessary. For the cheaper cuts, such as chuck, check the marinades on page 11.

Prior to tossing the steaks on the grill, take your fire poker and knock the gray ash off the briquettes. Move them around until the briquettes are 1 or 2 inches apart and adjust the grill so the fire is 4 or 5 inches below your steaks. Keep that spray bottle of water ready in case dripping juices cause the flame to flare up. When the juices come to the surface it's time to flip the steaks over with your long-handled tongs. Season the browned side; repeat when you turn it over for the final grilling.

# Mongolian Kabobs

2½ pounds round steak

¾ cup oil

½ cup soy sauce

2 tblsps Worcestershire sauce

1–2 cloves garlic, finely chopped

3 tblsps finely chopped fresh parsley

⅓ cup lemon juice

¼ tsp coarsely ground black pepper

1 large sweet green bell pepper, cut into 1½-inch cubes

12 small boiling onions

3 zucchini squash, cut into 1-inch slices

16 cherry tomatoes

pineapple chunks, one 13½-ounce can or fresh

Supposedly, it was the thundering hordes of Attila's horsemen who invented the clever shish kabobs, or meat and vegetables on a skewer grilled over a fire. Lamb, goat, or even horse was the meat of preference for the hungry conquerors. Lamb is still a favorite, but we Americans prefer tender chunks of beef, such as round or sirloin, partnered up with mushrooms, squash, cherry tomatoes, boiling onions (parboil for a few minutes first), bell pepper, or other veggies of choice. Use skewers with a square or flat surface; the food stays on better.

1. Cut the steak into 1-inch pieces.

2. In a bowl combine the oil, soy sauce, Worcestershire sauce, garlic, parsley, lemon juice, and pepper.

3. Place meat cubes in a glass or stainless bowl and pour marinade over all. Chill for 24 to 48 hours in refrigerator.

4. If you use bamboo skewers be sure to soak well before use.

5. Thread 8 12-inch skewers with alternating pieces of meat, vegetables, and pineapple. Use 4 chunks of meat on each skewer.

6. Grill 4 skewers at a time about 3 inches from coals for about 8 minutes per side. Turn as meat browns. Baste with your favorite sauce.

7. Continue grilling until all skewers of meat and vegetables are done.

8. Serve with Rice Pilaf.

Serves 6 to 8

# Steak Butter Sauce

As an alternative to barbecue sauce or marinade, try this butter sauce on a tender variety of steak.

In a small saucepan melt 1½ sticks of butter (not margarine!) and combine with ½ cup Worcestershire sauce. Simmer for 15 minutes. When your steaks are done to your taste, use a small brush and baste with this sauce before serving.

# Gaucho Steak Sauce

¼ cup oil (vegetable is okay)
¼ cup apple cider vinegar
3 tblsps finely chopped onion
½ tsp salt
½ tsp dry mustard
¼ tsp (one dash) nutmeg
¼ tsp mace
¼ tsp cloves
1 clove garlic, finely minced

**1.** In a small saucepan mix together the oil, vinegar, onion, salt, mustard, nutmeg, mace, cloves, and garlic. Bring to a simmer and cook for 5 minutes.

**2.** Offer sauce in a small pitcher or bowl. Pour over steak as desired.

## For Garlic Lovers

4 cloves garlic, peeled and finely chopped
1½ tsps salt
3 tblsps lemon juice
2 tsps Worcestershire sauce
¼ cup oil (vegetable is okay)

**1.** In a small bowl combine the garlic, salt, lemon juice, Worcestershire, and oil. Cover and refrigerate overnight if possible.

**2.** Brush over your beef shish kabobs, tender steaks or burgers just before you grill.

EASY BARBECUES

*for easy summer living*

# Purloined Sirloin

3 pounds boneless top sirloin steak, cut
    into 1½-inch cubes
¾ cup dry red wine
4 tblsps olive oil
3 cloves garlic, crushed
¼ tsp rosemary
¼ tsp thyme

**1.** Place meat in a glass bowl or baking dish.

**2.** In a small bowl mix together the wine, oil, garlic, rosemary, and thyme.

**3.** Pour marinade over meat. Cover and refrigerate at least 4 hours, preferably overnight.

**4.** Thread meat cubes on 6 or 8 skewers.

**5.** Grease the grill.

**6.** Cook skewered meat over a hot fire, turning and basting often with your favorite sauce. Medium rare takes about 15 minutes.

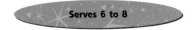

Serves 6 to 8

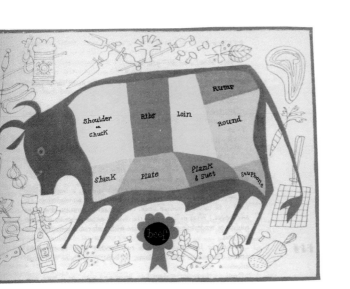

# Rice Pilaf

½ cup chopped onion
1 cup uncooked long-grain rice
¼ cup butter
1 tsp salt
1 tsp parsley
2 cups chicken broth

**1.** Using a heavy saucepan cook onion and rice in the butter until rice is golden brown.

**2.** Add in salt, parsley, and broth. Bring to a boil. Reduce heat, cover, and simmer for 20 minutes.

**Makes 6 servings**

# Coyote Canyon Skewered Beef

4 pounds boneless chuck roast

unsalted meat tenderizer

1½ cups pineapple juice (canned is okay)

1 cup dry red wine

1½ tsp Worcestershire sauce

1½ tblsps grated onion

3 cloves garlic, finely chopped or crushed

¾ tsp dry mustard

3 tblsps brown sugar

dash of cayenne pepper

¼ cup salad oil

¼ cup butter, melted

5 medium-sized ears of corn, husked and
   cut into 2-inch lengths

3 medium-sized green bell peppers,
   cut into 1-inch squares

2 large sweet onions, cut into
   1-inch chunks

**1.** Cut meat across grain and sprinkle with meat tenderizer according to package directions.

**2.** In a large glass bowl combine the juice, wine, Worcestershire, onion, garlic, mustard, brown sugar, and pepper. Set aside ⅓ cup of marinade.

**3.** Add meat to the bowl of marinade, stir meat around to cover. Cover chill overnight.

**4.** Remove meat from marinade and drain.

**5.** Thread meat onto skewers, alternating with corn, green pepper, and onion. Baste with butter sauce (see below)

**6.** Barbecue skewers of meat/veggies on lightly greased grill for about 4 to 6 minutes per side. Baste often with butter sauce.

## Butter Sauce

In a small bowl combine the oil, melted butter and reserved marinade. Use to baste your skewered beef and veggies.

In 1958 the California-grown artichoke had broken into the gourmet market from its once Monterey Bay home.

# The Chicken

Chicken is the queen of the barbecue table and versatile is her middle name. There are so many ways to cook chicken it's like an art form of its own. Don't get stuck in that barbecue rut of simply slapping the bird on the grill and mopping on the sauce from the supermarket shelf. Chicken deserves better and this section contains the flavorful answers.

# Laguna Beach Suntanned Chicken

4 good-sized boneless, skinless chicken breasts (about 1½ pounds)
½ cup vegetable oil
¼ cup lemon juice
1 tsp grated lemon peel
1 tsp dried basil leaves
3 medium cloves garlic, finely chopped
½ tsp salt
¼ tsp coarsely ground black pepper

**1.** In a shallow glass baking dish combine the oil, lemon juice, lemon peel, basil, garlic, salt, and pepper. Add in the chicken, turning over several times to coat with marinade. Refrigerate for 1 hour, turning chicken once.

**2.** Grill approximately 4 inches from medium-heat coals for 5 minutes per side. Poke with your turning fork to see that juices run clear.

Serves 4

# Cackle 'N' Shout Chicken

3 tblsps butter-flavored oil or shortening
3 medium cloves garlic, finely chopped
1 medium onion, chopped
1 can (8 ounces) tomato sauce
¼ cup bottled chili sauce
2 tblsps firmly packed brown sugar
2 tblsps Worcestershire sauce
1 tsp chili powder
½ tsp salt
½ tsp coarsely ground black pepper
1 2- to 3-pound fryer, cut up, or equal in legs and/or thighs

**1.** Place chicken pieces, skin-side down, on grill. The chicken should be about 6 inches above medium-hot coals. Grill the chicken 20 minutes, turning once.

**2.** Heat the oil or shortening in a medium-size saucepan over medium heat. Add in the garlic and onion and cook, stirring often, until the onion is clear but not brown. Stir in the tomato sauce, chili sauce, brown sugar, Worcestershire sauce, chili powder, salt, and pepper. Simmer for about 5 minutes to blend the flavors.

**3.** Baste the chicken generously with the sauce, turning often. Grill another 15 to 20 minutes or until juices run clear.

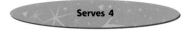
Serves 4

# High-Class Grilled Chicken Breasts

4 chicken breasts, skinned, rinsed
    and dried

¾ tsp coarsely ground black pepper

½ cup butter, melted

¼ cup fresh basil, finely chopped

½ cup butter or margarine, softened

1 tblsp grated Parmesan cheese

¼ tsp garlic powder

⅛ tsp salt

⅛ tsp coarsely ground pepper

**1.** Press the ¾ tsp pepper into the meaty side of the chicken pieces.

**2.** Combine the ½ cup melted butter with ¼ of the basil. Brush the chicken pieces with this mixture. Be generous.

**3.** In a separate bowl combine the ½ cup softened butter with 2 tablespoons of the basil, cheese, garlic, salt and pepper. Set aside.

**4.** Grill the chicken over medium coals for 8 to 10 minutes per side. Baste frequently with the melted butter/basil mixture.

**5.** Serve the chicken with small side bowls of the softened basil/butter sauce.

Serves 4

# Farmhand Hen

¾ cup vegetable oil

¼ cup melted butter

¼ cup lemon juice

2 tblsps brown sugar

1 tsp salt

¼ tsp coarsely ground black pepper

1 tsp paprika

3 tsps grated onion

2 medium cloves garlic, finely chopped

XX cup Tabasco sauce

¼ cup catsup

4 broilers, about 2½ pounds each, split lengthwise

**1.** In a medium bowl stir together the oil, butter, lemon juice, brown sugar, salt, pepper, paprika, onion, garlic, Tabasco, and catsup. Set aside ¼ cup of the sauce. Save the rest for later.

**2.** Baste the birds thoroughly with the ¼ cup sauce.

**3.** Grill the chickens, hollow side down, over coals. The coals must be white with ash, which means medium heat.

**4.** Cook for 20 minutes, brush with sauce, turn over.

**5.** Continue grilling for another 20 minutes, brushing with sauce often.

**6.** Chicken is done if you grasp the end of a leg and it moves easily. Also, if the juices run clear when you poke it with your turning fork.

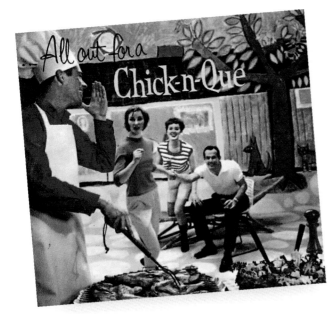

3-D glasses gave 1950s movies the appearance of depth and realism. Their inventor was scientist John F. Dreyer who made millions with his Polacoat company.

# Brother Ron's Chicken

This is really honestly my brother's version for barbecued chicken. He's a great cook and is known to be out there barbecuing something, anything, in a snowstorm in the middle of winter. A true dedicated grillmaster. Although he refuses to share his "secret" barbecue sauce concoction, this is more a method of cooking than an exact recipe.

**1.** Marinade chicken (legs and thighs are preferred) in one of the above smoky marinade mixes.

**2.** Grill chicken over your coals for about 5 minutes, or just until it gets a nice browning.

**3.** Pour about 3 cups of your favorite barbecue sauce into a large stainless steel bowl.

**4.** Add browned chicken into the bowl and toss about to cover with the sauce.

**5.** Place bowl over a low fire and cover the hood. Let simmer for about 15 minutes. Turn chicken about in the sauce once or twice.

**6.** Set bowl of chicken and sauce aside and remove each piece with tongs, let sauce drain off into bowl, then grill another minute or two to finish browning.

**7.** Hope you cooked enough as this is fantastic chicken! Tender, juicy, and flavorful.

# The Ham

Ham evokes memories of old-fashioned down-on-the-farm meals. It's folksy, well-loved, and can easily be dressed up with a wonderful variety of sauces to bath it in while slowly sizzling on the spit. This section also includes a fun and tropical method of preparing your next barbecued pork roast and pork chops that'll have them lining up for more.

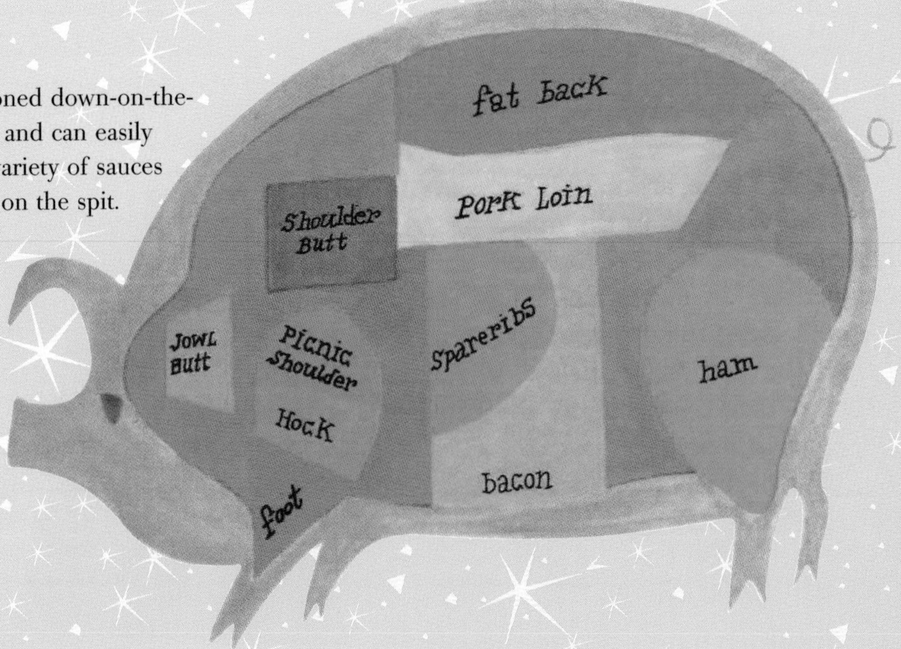

fat back

Pork Loin

Shoulder Butt

Jowl Butt

Picnic Shoulder

Spareribs

ham

Hock

foot

bacon

# Bee's Knees Ham Steak

½ cup honey

½ cup brown sugar

2 tblsps cornstarch

¼ cup pineapple juice (or orange juice or apricot nectar)

6 slices precooked lean ham, ½ inch thick

**1.** In a medium bowl mix together the honey and brown sugar. In a separate small saucepan mix together the cornstarch and juice. Stir over medium heat until the mixture thickens. Mix with the honey and sugar until sugar is melted and the sauce is well blended.

**2.** When the coals of the fire are covered with white ash they're ready.

**3.** If you have a nonstick enameled grill, slap the steaks on and grill about 10 minutes. Otherwise spritz the grill with nonstick spray.

**4.** Turn the ham steaks over and baste with the honey sauce.

**5.** Turn the steaks again, baste, and cook a few minutes longer. Ham is done when it appears shiny.

Serves 6 to 8

## Variation

**Mustard Glaze**

In a small bowl mix together ½ cup brown sugar, 2 tblsps flour, 1 tsp dry mustard. Before grilling rub into both sides of the ham steaks.

# Honey Dew Ham

Hopefully, you have all of the necessary equipment for spit barbecuing. This is an outstanding way to cook a good ham. Try doing it for one of your holidays, a yummy change from the usual baked ham dinner.

## Glaze

1 cup firmly packed brown sugar
¼ cup canned apricot nectar
½ cup honey

Combine the sugar, nectar, and honey, stirring over low heat until blended and sugar is dissolved.

**Makes 1½ cups**

Put ham on the spit. Place a shallow drip pan under the meat and turn on motor. Cook 10 minutes for each pound. Brush with above glaze often for the last 15 minutes.

# Drunken Ham

This ham isn't really tipsy, but the beer adds a great change in the flavor.

## Basting Sauce

½ cup flat beer
1 tblsp Worcestershire sauce
2 tblsps apple cider vinegar
2 tblsps honey
1 tblsp lemon juice
⅓ cup firmly packed brown sugar
⅔ cup bottled chili sauce

Combine beer, Worcestershire sauce, vinegar, honey, lemon juice, brown sugar, and chili sauce in a medium saucepan. Heat and stir until sugar is dissolved.

**Makes about 2 cups of sauce**

Prepare ham on the spit and turn on motor. Barbecue about 10 minutes per pound. Baste often with the sauce.

# Caribbean Pork Roast

2 tblsps olive oil

3 tblsps soy sauce

2 tblsps apple cider vinegar

2 tblsps water

1 tsp allspice

2 tsps sugar

2 tsps Thyme leaves

1 tsp cayenne pepper

1 tblsp minced onion (dried is okay)

½ tsp cinnamon

½ tsp nutmeg

1 boneless pork roast (about 3 pounds)

**1.** In a self-closing plastic bag or glass dish mix together the oil, soy sauce, vinegar, water, allspice, sugar, thyme, cayenne, onion, cinnamon, and nutmeg. Mix together well.

**2.** With a sharp cooking fork, poke 8 or 10 holes in the roast.

**3.** Add pork to the marinade and move it around in the bag or dish to coat well. Refrigerate overnight.

**4.** Remove meat and discard marinade.

**5.** Arrange the coals around outer edge of barbecue and place meat in the center of the grill. Close hood.

**6.** Cook 20 to 22 minutes per pound of roast. Meat thermometer should read 180°. Remove from grill and let stand 10 minutes before slicing.

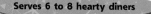

**Serves 6 to 8 hearty diners**

# Hickory Hill's Bestever Pork Chops

**4 tblsps soy sauce (the low sodium is okay)**

**4 tblsps lime juice**

**3 tblsps apricot preserves**

**1 tblsp Dijon-style mustard (I like honey Dijon)**

**1 large or 2 small cloves garlic, finely chopped**

**1 tsp grated lime peel**

**½ tsp grated lemon peel (optional)**

**4 boneless center-cut loin pork chops (about 1 inch thick)**

**1.** In a shallow glass dish combine the soy sauce, lime juice, preserves, mustard, garlic, and peel. Mix well.

**2.** Add in the pork chops and turn a couple of times to coat.

**3.** Cover the dish with plastic wrap and refrigerate for at least 2 hours before cooking.

**4.** Grill the chops over medium heat (about 5 inches from the coals) for 7 to 9 minutes per side. Use your meat thermometer.

When Lucille Ball and Desi Arnaz had a child of their own in 1957 the event was written into the script of their TV show.

# Boss Burgers

Ya gotta love 'em. Juicy, smoky, basted with the savory taste of a fine sauce and piled high with your favorite add-ons—perfection!

Offer the usual sliced tomatoes, good thick cheddar slices, sweet onion, pickles (see recipe for great homemade ones on page 99), lettuce (try using butterhead, or another alternative to the blah iceberg variety), avocado slices, sautéed mushrooms and/or onions, bleu cheese, cooked bacon strips, or use your imagination.

One more word:. Don't go for the cheapo buns for your burgers. If possible get those nice bakery ones, or try sourdough, or even thick-sliced rye.

# Drippin' Juicy Burgers

**1½ pounds lean ground beef**
**1 tblsp finely chopped onion**
**1 small can (⅔ cup) evaporated milk**
**2 tsps Worcestershire sauce**
**1 tsp salt**
**¼ tsp coarsely ground black pepper**
**1 tsp finely chopped fresh garlic**

**1.** In a medium-sized bowl mix together the beef, onion, milk, Worcestershire sauce, salt, pepper, and garlic.

**2.** Dampen your hands and shape the meat mixture into 8 patties.

**3.** Sear burgers over a hot fire, then raise grill (or spread out the coals) and continue grilling for another 8 minutes per side, or until juices run clear. Do not press with spatula as this presses out the juices.

**4.** Serve with your favorite array of toppings.

Serves 8

# San Andreas Fault(less) Burgers

**½ pound lean ground beef**
**½ pound lean pork sausage (also good with venison or elk sausage)**
**½ cup finely chopped green pepper**
**¼ cup finely chopped onion**
**2 eggs, slightly beaten**
**2 tsps finely chopped stuffed green olives**
**½ cup fine dry breadcrumbs**
**¼ cup water**

Combine the meats, pepper, onion, eggs, olives, breadcrumbs and water in a bowl. If you use game sausage add a little (1 tblsp) lard. Form into 6 patties. Grill over a medium flame, turning often. Grill buns and serve with your favorite accompaniments such as sliced tomatoes, lettuce, onion, etc.

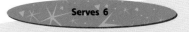
Serves 6

# Dixie's Jumbo Burgers

2 pounds ground beef (note: super-lean
    ground beef tends to get dry)

½ cup catsup

1 tsp salt

½ tsp coarsely ground black pepper

1 small onion, thinly sliced

½ pound smoked cheddar cheese, sliced

**1.** Divide meat into 10 equal portions. Place between sheets of waxed paper or plastic wrap and flatten into patties ½ inch thick and 4 inches across.

**2.** Spread 5 patties with the catsup. Season with the salt and pepper and place a slice of onion and cheese on each patty.

**3.** Top with the other 5 patties and pinch around the edges to seal. Be careful to make a good seal so the inside goodies don't leak.

**4.** Sear on grill and continue cooking for about 8 minutes on each side.

**Serves 5**

The best thing in 1956 travel was Greyhound's new Scenicruiser for "panoramic sightseeing."

# Rosarita Beach Burgers

2 tblsps beef lard (sorry, there's just no substitute for the taste)

2½ cups refried beans (canned is okay)

¼ cup finely chopped onion

1½ pounds ground beef

1 small onion, finely chopped

¼ cup dry breadcrumbs

1 egg, beaten

1 tsp Worcestershire sauce

¼ cup canned chopped green chilies, drained

½ tsp ground cumin

½ tsp salt

½ tsp chili powder

2 large tomatoes, thickly sliced

1 large ripe avocado, pitted, peeled, sliced

**1.** In a cast iron frying pan melt the lard. Add in the onion and cook over medium heat, stirring occasionally.

**2.** Add in the refried beans and simmer until heated through. Mash the beans with a potato masher. Set aside in a warm place.

**3.** In a medium bowl mix together the beef, the small chopped onion, breadcrumbs, egg, Worcestershire, green chilies, cumin, salt, and chili powder. Shape into 6 patties about ⅜ inches thick.

**4.** Sear patties over hot grill, then adjust the coals (or raise the grill) and continue cooking for another 8 minutes per side.

**5.** Grill burger buns. Place half of the bun on a plate and add a patty. Cover with a scoop of refried beans, a slice of tomato, then avocado. Serve open face or add other half of the bun. Messy, but oh so yummy!

Serves 6

Barbecue with that French's flavor

# Reuben Burgers

1½ pounds ground beef
½ tsp garlic powder
1 tsp salt
½ tsp coarsely ground pepper
6 slices lean bacon
1 small onion, finely chopped
1 16-ounce can sauerkraut, well drained
12 slices rye bread, thickly sliced
6 1-ounce slices Swiss cheese

**1.** In a medium bowl mix well the ground beef, garlic powder, salt, and pepper. Shape into 6 patties.

**2.** In a nice heavy skillet cook the bacon until crispy brown. Drain away all but one tablespoon of the fat. Pat the bacon with paper towels, crumble, and set aside.

**3.** Reheat the remaining bacon fat and add in the onion. Stir over medium heat until onion is clear but not brown. Add the sauerkraut, mix well with the onion, and stir until heated through. Keep warm.

**4.** Grill the patties about 8 minutes on each side. Check with your meat thermometer.

**5.** While burgers are cooking, toast the rye bread.

**6.** Place burger patty on a slice of toasted bread and top with the sauerkraut/onion mixture, crumbled bacon, and a slice of cheese before topping off with the remaining toast.

Serves 8

# Too-Good-To-Be-True Burgers

1 small sweet onion, peeled
1 carrot, washed and peeled
1 medium uncooked potato, peeled
1 cup dry breadcrumbs
1 pound ground beef
1 egg
1 tsp salt
¼ tsp coarsely ground pepper
½ tsp paprika
1 tsp finely chopped fresh parsley
¼ cup butter, melted

**1.** Put the vegetables through your food processor.

**2.** In a large bowl mix together the vegetables with the breadcrumbs, meat, egg, salt, pepper, paprika, and parsley.

**3.** Form into 8 patties. Grill. Baste occasionally with the butter.

Serves 8

# Park Ranger Burgers

1 tsp liquid smoke flavoring
1 egg, slightly beaten
1½ pounds ground beef
½ tsp salt
¼ tsp coarsely ground pepper

**1.** In a small bowl combine the liquid smoke and egg.

**2.** In a medium bowl combine the beef, egg mixture, salt, and pepper.

**3.** Form into 4 large or 6 small burgers. Grill and serve with your favorite toppings.

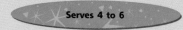
Serves 4 to 6

# Mustang Roundup Burgers

4 slices of lean bacon, cooked crisp and
    crumbled, reserving 2 tblsps bacon fat

¾ cup chopped onion

½ cup chopped green pepper

2 #303 cans of red kidney beans, drained

1 8-ounce can tomato sauce (for a change
    try one of the flavored variety)

2 tblsps chili powder

½ tsp salt

¼ tsp coarsely ground black pepper

1½ pounds ground beef

6 sourdough buns

1 cup grated sharp cheddar cheese

**1.** In a large skillet cook the onion and green pepper in the bacon fat until tender, but not browned. Drain

**2.** In the same skillet return the bacon, onion, green pepper, add beans, tomato sauce, chili powder, salt, and pepper. Simmer until heated, about 15 minutes. Stir often.

**3.** Form the ground beef into 8 burgers and grill as usual.

**4.** Toast buns on the grill. Place burgers on one half of the buns. Spoon on the bean mixture. Cover with cheese. Top with remaining half bun and serve.

Serves 8

By the mid-50's Americans were buying not only cars in bright colors, but appliances in pink, green, even crimson.

# Dogs

"Getcha steamin' hot Dachshunds!" What? Yep, these delights from our German friends were once called "Dachshunds" after the low-slung flop-eared canines. Then, a cartoonist named Tad Dorgan around 1906 started drawing Germans with their Dachshund dogs. Stadium hawkers at early baseball games started shortening the name of the German sausages from "Dachshund" to the favorite "hot-dog." Shortly thereafter an enterprising shoemaker, Nathan Handwerker, opened his own little hot dog stand at Coney Island. Soon, everyone had to have a Coney Island 'Dog after riding the famous roller coaster. Nathan's still exists right where it has since 1916.

Hot-dogs, franks, weenies, or tube steaks—whatever you call 'em—these little guys are a staple of picnics, cookouts, and barbecues. Easy to haul about, cheap, quick, and simple to cook, good hot-dogs can go a long way. Kids love 'em because they're no hassle to munch on. There's a wide variety of goodies to pile on, or be a purist and eat the juicy franks with basic mustard. Here are a few recipes to dress up the 'dogs.

# Cape Cod Beachside Dogs

hot dogs

mustard

sweet pickle relish (Oh, go on! make some of your own! See the recipe on page 99.)

baked beans

sweet onion, chopped (Walla Walla or Maui Sweet are best)

**1.** Slit each hot-dog halfway through lengthwise.

**2.** Spread a little mustard down the slit and a ½ teaspoon of relish.

**3.** Fill the slit of the hot-dog with baked beans and secure closed with dampened toothpicks.

**4.** Grill over medium heat, carefully moving so you don't lose the filling or burn the hot-dog.

**5.** Serve with more baked beans on the side and top with chopped sweet onion.

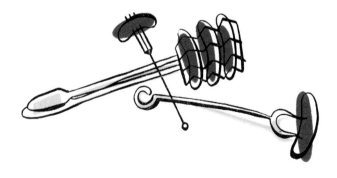

# Kauai Coast Franks

12 good quality frankfurters

1 large sweet onion (about 1 cup),
    finely chopped

3 tblsps vegetable oil

2 tblsps cornstarch

1 tblsp curry powder

¼ tsp ground allspice

1 tsp salt

2 cups canned crushed pineapple

2 tblsps apple cider vinegar

**1.** In a large skillet heat the oil and cook the onion until clear but not browned.

**2.** In a small bowl or cup mix together the cornstarch, curry, allspice and salt; stir into the onions and cook until thick and bubbly.

**3.** Stir in pineapple (with its syrup) and vinegar. Cook over low heat until mixture rethickens and starts to bubble.

**4.** Grill franks and baste with the pineapple sauce. When franks are done return to sauce and keep warm until served.

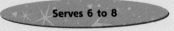

Serves 6 to 8

# Prairie Dogs

hot dogs
American cheese, sliced
sliced bacon

**1.** Slit the dogs halfway through, lengthwise.

**2.** Fill the slits with cheese, about ½ slice per dog.

**3.** Wrap the cheesed dogs with bacon, holding in place with dampened toothpicks.

**4.** Grill the dogs over medium coals, turning often, until bacon is done. Watch for flare-ups from the bacon fat. A wire mesh hot-dog basket works best for this.

**5.** Serve with your favorite barbecue sauce, baked beans, and maybe a green salad or coleslaw. Yum!

# Out-of-the-Net-and-into-th

# Fire (Fish)

L iving on a Pacific peninsula where fishing, both commercial and sport, is part of the lifestyle, I love fish. My personal favorite is the Pacific ling cod—one of the ugliest fish you could ever set eyes on. It seems like a third of the fish is a huge, nasty-looking head. But the steaks are firm, white, and just as delicious as halibut.

Be sure to grease the grill well before cooking any type of fish, unless it's in a basket or foil pouch. There's always a resounding groan when a big chunk of delicious ling cod or halibut sticks to the grill and falls through to the unforgiving fire. Also, use that nice big spatula to turn the fish. The key word is gently!

Fish fillets and steaks are wonderful barbecued. Fish cooks very quickly, about 12 minutes for a steak 1½ inches thick. Test with a fork, and if the fish flakes off it's done. Brush the steaks or fillets often with softened butter. You can add lemon juice, parsley, garlic, tarragon, dill, or other goodies to your basting butter.

Small fish, such as pan-sized trout, can be wrapped in heavy-duty foil and grilled without them falling through the grill. Try adding thinly sliced onion, mushrooms, green pepper, tomatoes, and/or bacon to the foil pouch before sealing well. Pouched fish takes about 15 minutes to cook.

You might also try sprinkling dried herbs on the coals to flavor your halibut, ling cod, or other favorite seafood. Herbs like bay, thyme, fennel, dill, or marjoram are great choices.

# Peninsula Grill

3 cloves garlic, finely chopped
¼ cup olive oil
dash of coarsely ground pepper
2 pounds firm type fish such as ling cod,
    halibut, tuna, or swordfish; cut into
    1½-inch chunks

**1.** In a large bowl combine garlic, oil, and pepper.

**2.** Add in fish chunks and gently toss to coat with oil/garlic mixture.

**3.** Thread fish chunks on 6 metal skewers.

**4.** Place skewers on a well-greased grill 4 to 6 inches above a hot fire.

**5.** Turn fish often and cook for 10 to 12 minutes. Fish is done if it flakes when poked with a fork.

**6.** Serve with the following spicy relish.

Serves 6

# Shipwreck Relish

3 small fresh or canned chilies, finely
    chopped
2 large ripe tomatoes, peeled, seeded,
    chopped
1 medium sweet onion, chopped
1 tsp sugar
3 tblsps red wine
½ tsp salt

**1.** In a medium glass bowl combine the chilies, tomatoes, onion, sugar, wine, and salt.

**2.** Cover and refrigerate overnight.

Makes about 3 cups

# Lighthouse View Halibut

**6 halibut steaks, about 1 inch thick**
**3 tblsps oil**

**1.** Rinse fish and pat dry. Brush with the oil.

**2.** Cook fish steaks 4 to 6 inches above coals on a well-greased grill.

**3.** Turn once, using a wide spatula, a total of about 8 to 10 minutes.

**4.** Serve with garlic/basil butter (see below)

Serves 6

# Garlic Butter for Fish

**2 cloves garlic, finely chopped**
**½ cup finely chopped fresh basil**
**½ cup butter, softened**
**dash of coarsely ground pepper**

**1.** In a small bowl combine the garlic, basil, butter, and pepper. Chill until ready to use. Serve with fish steaks.

America's love affair with the automobile leaped to sales of 7.9 million vehicles in 1955.

# Classic Salads on the Side

**C**heck out the zip of a bowl of chili, the snap of a good barbecue sauce, a juicy 'dog or burger cooked to perfection, and the perfect side dish is a salad. Whether it's a cool crispy green spinach salad next to your steak or a hill of potato salad, your plate will hold that perfect balance.

# Granny Green's Slaw

¾ cup mayonnaise

3 tblsps sugar

2 tblsp apple cider vinegar

1 tsp dry mustard

dash of celery salt

½ tsp salt

¼ tsp coarsely ground black pepper

8 cups shredded cabbage (a combination of red and green makes the dish more colorful)

½ cup finely chopped sweet onion (Walla Walla, Vidalia, or Maui Sweet are best)

½ cup shredded carrots

¼ cup finely chopped celery

**1.** In a bowl mix together the mayonnaise, sugar, vinegar, mustard, celery salt, salt, and pepper.

**2.** In a large bowl toss together the cabbage, onion, carrots, and celery.

**3.** Pour dressing mixture over vegetables and toss. This is best if refrigerated for a few hours or even overnight.

Makes about 8 cups

The '50s saw American teenagers become the major market for record sales. In 1953 album and single sales were $213 million. By 1959 they had leaped to over $600 million.

# Yankee Jack's Macaroni Salad

8 ounces small (salad) macaroni

¾ cup mayonnaise

½ tsp salt

3 tblsps sweet pickle relish

3 tblsps finely chopped sweet onion

½ cup thinly sliced celery

¼ cup finely chopped green pepper

1 cup baby peas

4 hard-boiled eggs, chopped

**1.** Cook the macaroni according to directions on the package. Drain well, rinse, and cool.

**2.** In a medium bowl mix together the mayonnaise, salt, pickle relish, and onion.

**3.** In a large bowl combine the cooled macaroni, celery, and green pepper.

**4.** Gently toss in the peas and eggs.

**5.** Chill well before serving.

Serves 6

# Country Cottage Slaw

½ cup mayonnaise

½ cup sour cream

3 tblsps apple cider vinegar

1½ tsp grated onion

½ tsp salt

½ tsp coarsely ground pepper

1 tsp poppy seed

6 cups finely shredded green cabbage
(for more color substitute 1 cup red
cabbage for the green)

2 cups apples, cored and diced (I like the
tangy sweet taste of Fuji, Gala, or
Gravenstein varieties)

½ cup chopped green pepper

**1.** In a medium bowl combine the mayonnaise, sour cream, vinegar, onion, salt, pepper, and poppy seed.

**2.** Toss together the cabbage, apples, and green pepper.

**3.** Combine the dressing with the cabbage mixture. Chill for several hours.

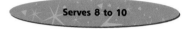

Serves 8 to 10

The average American could purchase their very own Volkswagen Beetle for $1,300 in the mid-50's.

# Second-Helping Potato Salad

9 cups potatoes, cooked, peeled, and cubed.
    Red potatoes are preferred, new whites
    are nice, good Russets will do.

1½ cups finely chopped celery

1 cup mayonnaise

1½ tblsps prepared mustard

½ cup finely chopped sweet onion

½ cup sweet pickle relish. (or finely chopped
    sweet pickles)

1 tsp salt

½ tsp coarsely ground black pepper

½ tsp paprika

½ tsp garlic powder

6 hard-boiled eggs, peeled and chopped

2 hard-boiled eggs for garnish

½ tsp paprika

1 nice bunch of fresh parsley (about 2 tblsps)

**1.** In a large bowl toss together the potatoes, celery, mayonnaise, mustard, onion, pickle, salt, pepper, paprika, and garlic. Gently toss in the eggs. Check for salt and pepper according to your taste.

**2.** Cover and chill at least one hour. Before serving, peel and slice the last 2 hard-boiled eggs and garnish along with the paprika and parsley.

**Serves 6 to 8**

# Milwaukee Spinach Salad

1 pound tender fresh small spinach leaves, washed and trimmed

6 slices lean bacon

4 green onions, finely chopped

1 clove garlic, crushed

½ cup apple cider vinegar (or you can try red wine vinegar)

½ tsp salt

¼ tsp coarsely ground black pepper

**1.** Pat spinach leaves dry and refrigerate.

**2.** In a heavy skillet cook bacon until all of the fat is rendered, 3 to 5 minutes. Drain on paper towels and reserve fat in the skillet. Cut bacon into small pieces.

**3.** Mound spinach in salad bowl.

**4.** Add onions and garlic to skillet and gently cook about 2 minutes over low heat.

**5.** Mix in vinegar, salt, and pepper. When mixture comes to a boil, pour over the spinach and sprinkle bacon bits over all.

**6.** Serve immediately.

Serves 6

# Sum-Sum-Summertime Salad

2½ cups raw spinach leaves, washed, torn into small pieces

1½ cups peeled and sliced cucumbers

½ cup thinly sliced sweet Walla Walla, Vidalia, or Maui onion

½ cup sliced radishes

2 cups small-curd creamed cottage cheese (1 pint)

paprika and minced parsley garnish

1 cup dairy sour cream

2 tsps lemon juice

½ tsp salt

¼ tsp coarsely ground pepper

**1.** In a large bowl toss together the spinach, cucumber, onion, and radishes. Arrange on four salad plates or in bowls.

**2.** Place a mound of cottage cheese in the center of each plate.

**3.** Sprinkle a little paprika and minced parsley over the cottage cheese to dress it up.

**4.** In a small bowl mix together the sour cream, lemon juice, salt, and pepper. Serve in a decorative small bowl on the side.

Serves 4 to 6

# Berliners' Favorite Hot Potato Salad

¾ cup lean diced bacon

1 cup chopped sweet onion

1 cup thinly sliced celery

3 tblsps flour

1⅓ cups water

⅔ cup apple cider vinegar

⅔ cup sugar

2 tsps salt

½ tsp coarsely ground pepper

8 cups potatoes, cooked, peeled,
   and cubed

**1.** In a large skillet brown the bacon. Drain on paper towels. Save ¼ cup of the fat and return to skillet.

**2.** Gently cook the onion and celery until clear but not brown. Drain on paper towels.

**3.** In the same skillet reheat the bacon fat and blend in the flour. Stir in the water and vinegar and continue stirring until mixture is thick and bubbly.

**4.** Stir in sugar, salt, pepper, and the cooked onion and celery.

**5.** Toss the dressing mixture with the potatoes and bacon.

**6.** Cover and bake at 350° for 30 minutes. Serve hot.

Serves 10 to 12

# Big Sur Bean Salad

1 can cut green beans

1 can red kidney beans

1 can (7 ounces) pitted black olives

2 cans (4 ounces) whole mushrooms

1 can (4 ounces) artichoke hearts

1 medium thinly sliced sweet onion

1½ cups sliced celery

**1.** Drain the beans, olives, mushrooms, and artichoke hearts and gently toss in a large bowl.

**2.** Toss in the onion and celery.

**Dressing**

½ cup salad oil or virgin olive oil

¼ cup tarragon vinegar

1 tsp salt

1 tsp sugar

1 tblsp fines herbes

¼ cup chopped fresh parsley

**1.** In a medium bowl mix together the oil, vinegar, salt, sugar, fines herbes, and parsley.

**2.** Gently toss dressing with vegetable mixture, cover and refrigerate overnight.

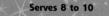
Serves 8 to 10

# Don't-Tell-The-Kids-It's-Healthy Pasta Salad

8 ounces spiral pasta

1 cup frozen peas

1½ cups cauliflower florets, washed, cut into bite-size pieces

1½ cups broccoli florets, washed, cut into bite-size pieces

1 pint cherry tomatoes, washed, cut in half

1 small red onion, thinly sliced (about ½ cup)

1 small sweet Walla Walla, or similar, thinly sliced (about ½ cup)

⅔ cup fresh mushrooms, thinly sliced

½ cup chopped sweet yellow or red ripe pepper

½ cup chopped celery

¼ cup chopped fresh parsley

1 bottle (8 ounces) of your favorite Italian dressing

**1.** Cook pasta according to package directions (don't overcook, should be firm). Drain, rinse, and cool.

**2.** Pour frozen peas into a sieve. Hold sieve over the sink and pour hot water over the peas. Drain and cool.

**3.** In a large bowl gently toss together the cauliflower, broccoli, tomatoes, onions, mushrooms, sweet pepper, celery, and parsley.

**4.** Mix in the peas last with the dressing. Refrigerate overnight.

Serves 8 to 10

The boom of car ownership and travel in the '50s brought the equal explosion in growth of motels.

# Breads

Crusty golden chunks of French bread or baguettes, tangy crispy-crackly sourdough, tender potato rolls—all are an outstanding accompaniment to that barbecue meal. And, let's be honest here—what could be better to sop up those wonderful juices from that T-bone, or as a pusher for those sweet yummy baked beans? Bread is definitely not low man on the barbecue totem pole. Test out these variations and see how bread can be the ultimate complement to your grillside gathering.

# Ultimate French

Slice a loaf of French bread, baguette, or sourdough lengthwise. Cut almost, but not all the way through, leaving the bread hinged. Open up loaf just enough to spread on butter (see seasoned butters below). Close up the loaf and wrap loosely in heavy grilling foil. Place on the back of your grill, or upper shelf if you have one, and heat for about 10 minutes. Turn once.

# Seasoned Butters and Other Bread Delights

**The car of the 1950s was the stuff of dreams and every American had the opportunity to own that dream.**

In a medium bowl cream ½ cup butter, then add in your seasoning and blend well. This makes enough for one loaf.

**1. Garlic 'n' Cheese Spread**—it's the most common, but try sprinkling Parmesan or another hard cheese over it.

**2. Smoky Joe Spread**—½ tsp liquid smoke

**3. Taos Spread**—½ tsp chili powder, 3 tblsps catsup, 2 cloves garlic (minced or pressed)

**4. Delft Spread**—¼ cup crumbled bleu cheese or Roquefort

**5. Seattle Style**—4 tblsps each of minced onion and fresh parsley

**6. Oysterville Herb**—½ tsp salt, ¼ tsp parsley, ¼ tsp paprika, ½ tsp dried thyme, dash of red pepper

# Scarborough's Fare Cornbread

12-inch cast iron skillet (Nothing else will
    do! Sorry!)

2 cups cornmeal

¼ cup sugar

1 tsp salt

2 eggs, well beaten

1 cup sweet milk

1 cup sour milk combined with 1 tblsp
    vinegar and 1 tsp baking soda
    or 1 cup buttermilk

¼ cup butter

1 more cup sweet milk

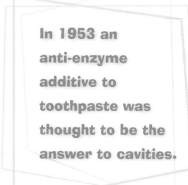

In 1953 an anti-enzyme additive to toothpaste was thought to be the answer to cavities.

**W**hile my husband was in Vietnam, two of his Marine Corps pals helped me take care of our horses. One of the guys, Gene Scarborough, also liked to cook and shared some of his family's favorite recipes. Thanks, Gene.

**1.** Preheat oven to 350°.

**2.** In a medium bowl mix together the cornmeal, sugar, salt, eggs, 1 cup sweet milk, and the cup of sour milk (with the vinegar and soda).

**3.** Melt butter in the cast iron skillet, swirling the butter around to grease the sides. Remove from heat.

**4.** Turn cornmeal batter into the skillet, then pour the last cup of sweet milk over the top. Do not stir.

**5.** Bake for 1 hour or until butter knife comes out clean when inserted into the center. Bread will be moist.

# New England Johnnycake

1¼ cups sifted flour

¾ cup yellow cornmeal

1 tblsp baking powder

¼ cup sugar

½ tsp salt

2 eggs, beaten

1 cup heavy cream

**1.** Preheat oven to 425°.

**2.** In a medium bowl sift together the flour, cornmeal, baking powder, sugar, and salt.

**3.** Add in the beaten eggs and cream. Beat until smooth (use your mixer if you like).

**4.** Pour into a 9-inch square baking pan and bake about 30 minutes.

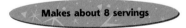

**Makes about 8 servings**

# Featherbed Potato Rolls

This great recipe is over 100 years old. I always make a double batch so I can send some home with friends and family.

1 medium-sized potato
1 envelope dry yeast
¼ cup warm water
⅓ cup sugar
1 tsp salt
¼ cup butter (not margarine or shortening)
1 egg, beaten
4½ cups flour
3 tblsps butter, melted

**1.** Peel potato, cover with water in a small saucepan and cook until done.

**2.** Remove potato and mash. Save 3/4 cup of the potato water.

**3.** Dissolve yeast in ¼ cup warm water; cool to lukewarm.

**4.** In a medium bowl mix together the sugar, salt, and ¼ cup butter. Stir in the reserved potato water.

**5.** Mix together the yeast mixture, mashed potato, egg, and 2 cups of the flour; stir or beat with your mixer until smooth.

**6.** Add in remaining 2½ cups of flour and mix well.

**7.** Knead dough on a lightly floured board until smooth and satiny looking.

**8.** Place dough in a well-greased large bowl; turn dough to grease all sides.

**9.** Cover with a clean dishcloth or cheesecloth, and set in a warm place until dough has doubled in size. I turn on the oven for a couple of minutes, turn it off, and set dough inside.

**10.** Punch dough down (my grandsons love doing this!) and shape into 24 balls.

**11.** Place a dozen of the dough balls into 9-inch layer pans. Brush with that last bit of melted butter and let rise again until doubled.

**12.** Bake in a preheated oven at 375° for 20 minutes or until very light brown.

**13.** Serve with lots of butter, honey-butter, jam, or preserves. We have also used these as hamburger buns.

# Gramma Moretti's Famous Pizza Bread

1 package dry yeast

1½ cups warm water

1 8-ounce can spaghetti sauce
(or homemade without meat)

1 tblsp sugar

3 tblsps grated Parmesan cheese

1½ tsps garlic powder

½ tsp leaf oregano (or fresh is really nice)

½ tsp sweet basil (fresh is much better)

3 tblsps virgin olive oil (or regular if you
like more flavor)

6¾ to 7 cups all-purpose flour

**1.** In a large bowl dissolve yeast in the warm water.

**2.** Stir in sauce, sugar, cheese, garlic, oregano, basil, and olive oil.

**3.** Add in the flour a little at a time, mix well.

**4.** Knead on floured board for 5 minutes until dough is smooth.

**5.** Place dough in large well-greased bowl, turning once to grease it all over.

**6.** Let rise in a warm place until dough is doubled.

**7.** Divide dough into 3 parts; shape each part into a 12-inch loaf. Please on greased cookie sheet.

**8.** Let dough rise again until doubled.

**9.** Bake in a preheated oven at 375° for 30 to 35 minutes or until golden brown.

**10.** Remove loaves from cookie sheet; cool. Brush crust with melted butter.

**11.** Serve in thick slices; we like it toasted on the grill. Slather with garlic/parsley butter.

The favorite entertainment at neighborhood parties were games such as charades, balloon bounce, suitcase race, and drawing in the dark.

# Relishes, Pickles, & all the Trimmings

'Dogs aren't 'dogs without the delectable flavor of a great relish. The stuff they sell in the stores comes from . . . well . . . I've never quite figured out where! But, wait until you slap down a bowl of your own homemade and you'll never drive down that supermarket aisle again. Relishes, pickles, chutneys, and special sauces like these are like the ribbon on a birthday present.

# C-Bar Ranch Relish

3 large ripe (but not soft) tomatoes, peeled, seeded, finely chopped
1 sweet red or yellow pepper (about 1 cup) finely chopped
½ cup finely chopped celery
1 small sweet onion (about ⅔ cup) finely chopped
3 tblsps apple cider vinegar
2 tblsps sugar
½ cup cold water
1 tsp salt
dash coarsely ground pepper

**1.** In a medium bowl combine the tomatoes, pepper, celery, onion, vinegar, sugar, water, salt, and pepper. Chill overnight. Drain well and serve.

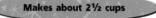
Makes about 2½ cups

By the end of the 1950s Americans were spending $12 billion per year on tools for do-it-yourself projects.

# Granny's Red and Green Relish

1 cup chopped ripe tomatoes
½ cup finely chopped celery
½ cup finely chopped green pepper
½ cup finely chopped sweet onion
1 tsp salt
3 tblsps apple cider vinegar
¼ tsp dry mustard
2 tblsps oil

**1.** Put the tomatoes, celery, green pepper, and onion in a colander and let drain for a few minutes.

**2.** Place the vegetables in a large bowl.

**3.** In a small bowl combine the salt, vinegar, mustard, and oil. Add to the vegetables and toss.

**4.** Spoon mixture into a glass jar and cover tightly. Store in refrigerator for 2 or 3 days before serving with meat.

Makes about 1 pint

# Pinkslipper Pickled Peaches

1 can (30 ounces) peach halves
2 tblsps red hot cinnamon candies
½ cup apple cider vinegar
½ cup sugar
dash (⅛ tsp) ground allspice
1 piece (about 3" long) stick cinnamon
whole cloves

**1.** Drain and set aside peaches, saving 1 cup of the syrup.

**2.** In a saucepan combine the syrup, candies, vinegar, sugar, allspice and cinnamon. Bring mixture to a simmer and cook for 3 or 4 minutes or until sugar dissolves. Stir constantly.

**3.** Stud each peach half with 4 or 5 of the whole cloves.

**4.** Place peaches in a screw-top jar, quart size, and pour syrup over them.

**5.** Cool and cover jar with a tight lid. Refrigerate at least overnight before serving.

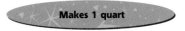

Makes 1 quart

# Farmhouse Harvest Relish

1 cup unpeeled cored and chopped
    tart apples
¾ cup shredded green cabbage
½ cup finely chopped celery
3 tblsps finely chopped green pepper
4 tsps chopped pimiento (optional, but
    adds some nice color)
3 tblsps apple cider vinegar
⅓ cup sugar
½ tsp salt
¼ tsp ground allspice

**1.** In a bowl toss together the apples, cabbage, celery, green pepper, and pimiento.

**2.** In a small bowl combine the vinegar, sugar, salt, and allspice. Toss with the apple mixture.

**3.** Spoon relish into a pint-size jar and cover tightly. Refrigerate at least overnight before serving.

Makes 1 pint

# Indiana Annie's Corn Relish

1 can (12 ounces) whole kernel corn, drained
½ cup finely chopped celery
3 tblsps finely chopped green pepper
2 tblsps finely chopped pimiento
3 tblsps finely chopped sweet onion
½ tsp salt
¾ cup olive oil
¼ cup wine vinegar
¼ tsp coarsely ground black pepper
¾ tsp paprika

**1.** In a bowl toss together the corn, celery, green pepper, pimiento, onion, and salt.

**2.** In a separate bowl combine the olive oil, vinegar, pepper, and paprika. Toss with the veggies.

**3.** Spoon into a screw-top jar and refrigerate for at least 24 hours before serving.

Makes about 1 pint

When Disneyland opened on July 17, 1955, studio publicists issued 20,000 tickets to the press, employees, and Hollywood stars.

# My Bestever Champion Burger Relish

2 sticks (2 inches long) cinnamon

2 tsps whole cloves, crushed with a knife

2 tsps whole allspice, also crushed

1 quart apple cider vinegar

4 cups ripe, but firm, peeled, seeded, and
coarsely chopped tomatoes

2 cups white sugar

¼ tsp cayenne pepper

4 tsps mustard seed

4 cups unwaxed, unpeeled, coarsely chopped
cucumbers

1½ cups cored, seeded, and chopped green
bell pepper

1½ cups seeded and chopped sweet ripe
(red or yellow) bell pepper

1 cup chopped celery

1½ cup chopped sweet onion

½ cup pickling salt
(not the iodized kind)

1½ tblsps ground turmeric

2 quarts cold water (use
bottled if yours is high
in minerals or
chlorine)

If I say so myself, this is scrumptious relish. I usually make lots of extra to take along to barbecues and to give away to its avid fans.

**1.** Cut a 6 inch square of cheesecloth; place the cinnamon, cloves and allspice in the center and tie with string into a little pouch .

**2.** In a nonaluminum or cast iron pan drop the spice bag into the vinegar and bring to a boil. Turn down heat and simmer for 15 minutes, uncovered.

**3.** Retain the spice bag and add in the tomatoes. Bring this back to a boil, then turn down to a simmer and cook for about 30 minutes. The mixture should look like a puree.

**4.** Stir in the sugar, cayenne, and mustard seed. Pour into a bowl and let stand overnight.

**5.** Next combine the cucumbers, peppers, celery, and onion. Be sure to use a glass or stainless bowl. Sprinkle the salt and turmeric over the vegetables and pour in the cold water. Mix gently, cover, and refrigerate overnight.

**6.** Wash and sterilize 7 half-pint canning jars and lids.

**7.** Drain the salty water from the vegetables and add in enough cold water to cover again. Let the veggie mixture set for 1 hour, then drain in a colander. Use a clean jar or potato masher and gently press more of the liquid out of the vegetables.

**8.** Reheat the tomato and vinegar mixture to a gentle boil over medium heat. Add the drained veggies and bring mixture back to a boil. Cook uncovered for about 5 minutes. Stir often.

**9.** Remove relish from heat and throw away the spice bag.

**10.** Ladle relish while it's hot into your hot canning jars. Leave ½-inch head space. Wipe rims clean and attach lids. Process in a boiling water bath for 10 minutes.

**Makes 7 yummy half-pints**

# The Brits' Hot 'n' Spicy Chutney

10 cups peeled and chopped ripe tomatoes

6 cups peeled and chopped tart apples (like Granny Smith)

2 large sweet onions (about 2 cups), chopped

1 box (15 ounces) seedless raisins

2 cloves garlic, finely chopped

1 pound (2 cups) dark brown sugar

1 tblsp salt

1 tblsp ground cinnamon

2 tsps crushed dried red peppers

1 tsp ground allspice

½ tsp ground ginger

½ tsp ground cloves

2 cups apple cider vinegar

Don't get scared off by something new. Chutney is just another version of a great accompaniment to meat. Give it a try.

**1.** In a large kettle, combine all ingredients.

**2.** Simmer mixture 45 minutes, stirring often, or until chutney is thickened.

**3.** Ladle into sterilized canning jars; seal with lids. Process according to manufacturer's directions.

# Mexicali Guacamole

3 avocados, cubed

1 clove fresh garlic, finely chopped

2 tblsps extra virgin olive oil

1 tblsp lemon juice

¼ cup salsa (mild or hot, whatever you prefer)

salt and pepper to taste

Okay, so let's move on to the dippies and other enticing appeteasers. My problem is trying to keep from stuffing up on these choice goodies while the main course is fragrantly grilling over the mesquite blaze.

Take note here that true guacamole is not mashed into goop. It is chopped into small cubes like your salsa ingredients.

**1.** In a medium bowl mix together the avocados, garlic, olive oil, lemon juice, salsa, salt and pepper. Chill for at least 1 hour.

**2.** Serve with warm tortilla chips.

# Snappin' Sweet Pickles

7 pounds cucumbers, washed and cut into
    ¼-inch slices
2 gallons cold water
2 cups dehydrated lime (canning type)
6 cups apple cider vinegar
9 cups sugar
1 tsp celery salt
1 tsp pickling spices
1 tsp mustard seed
2 tsps salt
1 tsp whole cloves

**1.** Put the sliced cukes into a large stainless steel bowl; cover with the 2 gallons of water and lime. Mix gently.

**2.** Leave cukes to set in a cool place for 24 hours. Stir occasionally.

**3.** Drain cukes and rinse well.

**4.** Cover cukes with more cold water and let set for another 3 hours.

**5.** Drain well.

**6.** In a large saucepan or pot remaining ingredients. Bring to a gentle simmer and stir until sugar is dissolved.

**7.** Let syrup mixture cool, pour over the cukes.

**8.** The next morning bring the cukes and syrup to a gentle boil and cook for about 25 minutes or until cukes become transparent.

**9.** Pack in sterilized canning jars, seal with lids and process in boiling water bath for 10 minutes.

*Let's have a Bar-B-Q!*

**YOU can enjoy this grill-rotisserie**

Lipton Soups put their famous "California Onion Soup Mix" on the market in 1954. Chips and dip were never the same again.

# Que Bueno Salsa

8 to 10 large ripe tomatoes, peeled, seeded, and chopped

2 large sweet onions

4 to 5 sweet yellow or red bell peppers

2 small cans diced mild green chilies

½ cup apple cider vinegar

1 6-ounce can tomato paste

1 tblsp salt

2 large cloves garlic

2 tsps red chili powder

2 tblsps cilantro

½ tsp oregano

**1.** Coarsely chop the tomatoes, onions, and peppers in a food processor.

**2.** In a large stainless pot add in the chopped veggies, the chilies, vinegar, tomato paste, salt, garlic, chili powder, cilantro, and oregano.

**3.** Bring to a gentle boil, then turn down to simmer. Cook for 30 minutes.

**4.** Fill sterilized canning jars, wipe top rim clean and seal. Process in a boiling water bath for 15 minutes.

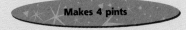

Makes 4 pints

# O'Boy Apples

1 cup honey (try to get a local variety as it has more flavor)

¼ cup apple cider vinegar

2 tblsps butter (not margarine)

3 cups peeled, cored, and thinly sliced apples. I prefer Gala, Fuji, Braeburn or Gravenstein varieties.

This can be served chilled or hot; as a dessert (with cream or vanilla ice cream), or as a side dish with pork or ham.

**1.** In a large saucepan heat together the honey, vinegar, and butter.

**2.** When liquid is bubbling gently, add in the apple slices and toss gently.

**3.** Simmer until apple slices are tender and semitransparent. Be careful they don't stick and scorch.

# Poodle Springs Sauce

6 cooking apples such as Gravenstein or
  Granny Smith
3 ripe (but not mushy) Bartlett or Bosc
  pears
3 tblsps water
1 2-ounce package cinnamon red-hot
  candies

**1.** Peel, core, and slice the apples and pears.

**2.** Place fruit in a heavy saucepan with a tight-fitting lid.

**3.** Add water to the fruit and simmer over low heat, covered, until fruit is tender. Takes about 30 minutes. Stir occasionally to keep it from sticking.

**4.** Remove from heat and stir in candies until they dissolve.

**5.** Cool if desired, then refrigerate. Or serve hot. Makes a great side dish to ham or pork dishes.

Behavioral Science took a stab at controlling the TV audience by experimenting with subliminal advertising.

# Get Your Just Desserts

Frankly, after all the delights off of the grill it's tough to find room for even a thin slice of cake or other goody. But, maybe after sitting by the lake or around the campfire you'll find some space for something sweet and delectable. Here are a few ideas to finish off a special event, celebration, or get-together.

# Gimme-Another-Slice Apple Pie

**Old-fashioned perfect pie crust (recipe follows)**

**Filling**

6 large cooking apples, such as Pippin or
    Granny Smith (5 cups)
1 tblsp lemon juice
¾ cup sugar
1½ tblsps cornstarch
1 tsp ground cinnamon
dash of nutmeg
white of one egg, beaten with
    1 tablespoon water
1 tblsp butter, cut into small pieces

**1.** Preheat oven to 450°.

**2.** Prepare crust according to recipe on page 113.

**3.** Peel, core, and slice the apples ¼-inch thick. Toss in a large bowl with the lemon juice.

**4.** Add into the apples the sugar, cornstarch, cinnamon, and nutmeg. Toss gently.

**5.** Brush the pie shell with the egg/water mixture.

**6.** Spoon in the apple mixture. Dot the apples with chips of butter.

**7.** Cover apple mixture with the top crust following directions on page 113.

**8.** Place on center rack and reduce heat to 350°. Bake 1 hour to 1 hour 15 minutes or until crust is lightly browned and filling is bubbling out of the crust slits.

**9.** Cool pie on wire rack until just warm. Serve with a fat slice of good cheddar cheese (if you're a Northwesterner you know that's Tillamook! Yum!), a big glop of whipped cream, or a spoonful of vanilla ice cream.

Serves 6 to 8

# Old-Fashioned Perfect Pie Crust

2 cups all-purpose flour
½ tsp salt
¾ cup butter-flavored shortening or lard
    (cut into small chunks)
approximately 5 tblsps ice water

The Good Housekeeping seal of approval was given to the '50s necessity, the folding TV tray sold for $2.95 by Cal-Dak.

**1.** In a medium bowl mix the flour and salt.

**2.** If you have a food processor pour in the flour mixture and mix with the shortening. Use the pulse speed until the mixture looks like coarse crumbs. If you don't have a processor use your hands and crumble it all together.

**3.** Run the processor on low, add the ice water a little at a time and process just until the dough sticks together. If it seems too dry add another tablespoon of water. If you're doing this by hand use a large wooden spoon.

**4.** Divide the dough into 2 balls. Wrap in clear plastic wrap and refrigerate at least 1 hour.

**5.** Roll out the dough into two 10-inch "pancakes." The dough should be about ⅛ inch thick. Fold each into halves, then quarters, so you can transport it to the pie pan.

**6.** Unfold crust in pan and trim to about 1 inch wider than the edge.

**7.** Baste bottom crust with egg/water mixture and spoon in the apples.

**8.** Add top crust and pinch edges together. Make a fluted edge by pinching the dough between your fingers every inch.

**9.** Cut slits in the top or get fancy and cut designs.

# Astoria's Chocolate Cake

1 cup sugar
2 cups flour
1 cup cold coffee
4 tblsps powdered cocoa
2 tsp baking powder
1 cup mayonnaise

Astoria, Oregon, was founded by the pioneer fur traders and fishermen. This charming small city clings to the steep sides of a forested point of land at the end of the bountiful but dangerous Columbia River. The streets struggle at dizzying angles past block after block of Victorian-era "ladies" (houses). Once in a while, as you drive parallel to the town, there's a glimpse of river traffic on its way from Asia and other exotic ports. Enormous car carriers, bulky, awkward, ugly, and practical, churn past the elegant masts of an antique sailing ship "parked" at the maritime museum. Astoria, named after fur trader king John Astor, is a town with all kinds of restaurants and remarkable food. This moist plenteous cake is named after my favorite place.

**1.** In a medium bowl combine the sugar, flour, coffee, cocoa, baking powder, and mayonnaise.

**2.** Grease and flour a 9 x 9-inch baking pan.

**3.** Bake at 350° for approximately 30 minutes. Test center with a toothpick or butter knife. If it comes out clean the cake is done.

**4.** I've always served this with whipped cream or vanilla ice cream and left off the icing. The cake is very moist and rich.

HOW TO BUILD THEM
HOW TO USE THEM

# Take-It-Easy Picnic Cake

This is a delicious moist cake with a couple of shortcuts to make it a little easier.

**1 package (18-ounce) yellow cake mix**
**1 package (3-ounce) instant vanilla pudding**
**4 eggs**
**¾ cup sherry**
**¾ cup oil**

**The first TV dinner was invented by the Swanson Frozen Food Company in 1954.**

**1.** In a large bowl combine cake mix, pudding mix, eggs, sherry and oil.

**2.** Beat with your mixer at medium speed for 4 or 5 minutes.

**3.** Pour batter into 9 x 13-inch greased baking pan and bake at 350° for 35 to 45 minutes. Test for doneness with toothpick.

**4.** Cool and frost with following recipe:

## Broiled Frosting

**1 cup brown sugar**
**⅓ cup butter, softened**
**⅓ cup evaporated milk**

**1.** Combine sugar, butter, and milk in a small bowl. Spread evenly over cooled cake.

**2.** Place cake about 5 inches below broiler and toast for about 4 minutes or until golden brown.

**Cake serves about 12 to 14**

# Knock-Your-Sox-Off Carrot Cake

2 cups flour

¼ cup yellow cornmeal

2 cups sugar

1 tsp salt

3 tsps baking soda

1 tsp baking powder

2 tsps cinnamon

3 large eggs

1½ cups peanut oil

2 cups finely grated fresh carrots

2 tsps vanilla extract

1 cup crushed pineapple

½ cup finely chopped dried apricots

½ cup chopped walnuts

1½ cups flaked coconut

**1.** In a large bowl combine the flour, cornmeal, sugar, salt, soda, baking powder, and cinnamon.

**2.** In a separate bowl beat together the eggs and oil until smooth.

**3.** Gradually add the dry ingredients to the egg mixture.

**4.** Fold in the carrots, vanilla, pineapple, apricots, nuts, and coconut.

**5.** Pour into 2 greased and floured loaf pans and bake at 350° for 60 minutes. Let cool before frosting (recipe to follow).

## Cream Cheese Frosting

¾ cube butter, softened

1½ cups powdered sugar

1 8-ounce package of cream cheese, softened

1 tblsp lemon juice

¾ cup flaked coconut

½ cups chopped walnuts

**1.** In a medium bowl beat together the butter, sugar, cream cheese, and lemon juice.

**2.** Fold in the coconut and walnuts.

**3.** Frost cooled cake.

**The first rock and roll concert was put on by Cleveland disc jockey, Alan Freed, in March 1952.**

# Snoqualmie Falls Tipsy Peaches

4 ripe peaches
8 whole cloves
2 tblsps butter
½ cup sugar
1 tsp ground cinnamon
¼ cup brandy

**1.** Dip peaches in boiling water and hold for 10 seconds or until skin slips off. Chill immediately in a bowl of ice water. Drain quickly and peel right away before peaches start to brown.

**2.** Halve the peaches, remove the pit and stick one whole clove in the bottom of the halves.

**3.** Brush outside of peach halves with the melted butter. Sprinkle sugar in each half and follow with a light sprinkle of cinnamon.

**4.** Fill each peach half with a spoonful of brandy and any remaining butter.

**5.** Place peach halves directly on the grill over a medium fire. Halves are done when the bottom turns light brown. Serve with a dollop of whipped cream if you like.

Serves 4

In 1955 the McDonald brothers sold their hamburger stand to milk-shake machine maker Ray Kroc, and an American institution was born.

# Snow Moose

²/₃ cup boiling water

2 envelopes unflavored gelatin

½ cup sugar

1 tsp vanilla extract

1 cup evaporated milk

¼ tsp ground cinnamon

2 cups ice cubes

Your choice of fresh fruit or berries

**1.** Pour the hot water and gelatin into a blender. Process on high speed for 30 seconds

**2.** Pour in sugar and process 5 seconds more.

**3.** Add in vanilla, milk, cinnamon, and ice and process 2 minutes more or until mixture is smooth.

**4.** Pour into individual dessert dishes and chill at least 1 hour.

**5.** Top with your favorite fruit or fresh berries.

Serves 6

1956 and 1957 the adult portion of the entertainment public hoped that singer Pat Boone would take over Elvis's crown. Pat was wholesome, safe, and didn't have sideburns.

# Tropic-of-Cancer Fruity Dessert

6 ripe but firm bananas

6 tblsps brown sugar

6 tblsps butter, melted

2 tblsps ground cinnamon

½ cup toasted flaked coconut (see below)

⅔ cup chocolate syrup

vanilla ice cream or frozen yogurt

**1.** Preheat grill.

**2.** Peel bananas, save half of the skin.

**3.** Slice each banana lengthwise and return to the saved skin.

**4.** In a small bowl mix together the sugar, butter, and cinnamon.

**5.** Place each banana (still in skin half) on a square of heavy-duty foil.

**6.** Spoon the sugar mixture over each banana and wrap tightly in the foil.

**7.** Grill foil packages over medium fire for 100 minutes.

**8.** Remove from grill, open packets, and transfer bananas to individual dessert dishes.

**9.** Top with ice cream, chocolate, and coconut.

Serves 6

## Toasted Coconut

Spread coconut over a shallow baking sheet and bake at 350° for 12 to 15 minutes or until lightly browned.

# Fruit-on-a-Stick

Those skewers work well for a delicious dessert of grilled fruit. Cook over a medium flame, turning often (carefully!), until lightly browned.

Try the following combinations or match up your favorites:

**1.** Pineapple chunks (fresh is best if possible), dipped in ginger, grilled, then dipped in toasted shredded coconut.

**2.** Pineapple chunks dipped in butter, grilled, and basted with rum.

**3.** Pineapple chunks, alternating with banana pieces, basted with honey butter.

**4.** Apple chunks, basted with melted butter and sprinkled with cinnamon.

**5.** Apple chunks alternating with pineapple and basted with melted butter mixed with brandy. Or baste with brandy and serve flambé style.

**6.** Banana chunks alternating with orange segments and firm pear, basted with honey butter.

1953 saw the hit comedy movie, *Long Long Trailer*, starring Lucy and Desi Arnaz. Their rolling home featured all sorts of kitchen gadgets.

# Thirst Quenchers

The blistering summer sun is disappearing into that perfect barbecue time of the evening. Your guests are relaxing around the savory smoke watching the burgers sizzle. This is the time to break out that great Melamine tray with its dancing veggies and serve up the drinks. Sure, the smell of that great chow will make their mouths water, but an ice cold glass of one of these thirst quenchers will keep them happy until it is time to pass around the plates.

# Big Island Punch

2 cups (16 ounces) pineapple juice

1 can (6 ounces) frozen orange juice

4 cups (32 ounces) guava or mango juice combination

1 can (6 ounces) frozen lemonade concentrate

1 bottle (2 liters) ginger ale

3 tsp coconut extract flavoring

5 tsps rum extract flavoring

dash of ground allspice

**1.** Chill all juices and ginger ale beforehand.

**2.** In a large punchbowl mix together the pineapple juice, orange juice, tropical juice blend, lemonade, and ginger ale. Mix well.

**3.** Serve over crushed ice. Keep punch cold by placing it in a bed of more crushed ice.

**4.** For decoration you can float slices of orange or similar fruit.

Serves 16 (1-cup servings)

# San Simeon Sunset Tea

8 tea bags (regular orange/pekoe) or
    8 teaspoons loose tea

2 cups boiling water

2 cups sugar

2 cups cold water

2 cups fresh lemon juice

1 large banana, sliced

1 cup fresh strawberries, hulled and sliced

2½ cups fresh pineapple chunks
    (canned is okay)

2 large navel oranges, cut into slices

2 cups melon (honeydew, cantaloupe or
    similar, but not watermelon as it gets
    too mushy), carved into balls or
    chunks

1 bottle ( 28 ounces) ginger ale

**1.** Steep the tea in boiling water for 3 to 5 minutes; strain and mix in the sugar. Stir until sugar is dissolved.

**2.** Add cold water and lemon juice to tea mixture and chill.

**3.** Just before serving pour tea into a nice punchbowl and add in fruit.

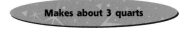

Makes about 3 quarts

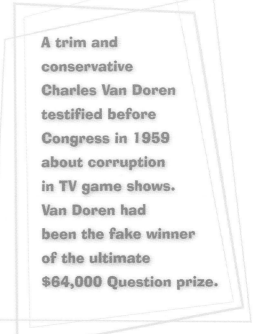

A trim and conservative Charles Van Doren testified before Congress in 1959 about corruption in TV game shows. Van Doren had been the fake winner of the ultimate $64,000 Question prize.

# Kansas City Razzleberry Punch

3 (3-ounce) packages red raspberry gelatin

4 cups boiling water

1½ cups sugar

4 cups cold water

2¼ cups orange juice (fresh or frozen)

1½ cups lemon juice

½ cup lime juice

1 quart ginger ale

2 (10-ounce) packages frozen raspberries

**1.** In a large bowl dissolve packages of gelatin in boiling water.

**2.** Stir in the sugar until dissolved. Mix in the cold water and juices.

**3.** Cool, but do not refrigerate or the gelatin will thicken.

**4.** When you're ready to serve, pour the juice mixture into a punchbowl and stir in the ginger ale and frozen raspberries. Stir until the berries are broken apart.

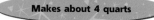

Makes about 4 quarts

# Index